PAUL and MORGAN HAMM

Olympic Heroes

**An
Unauthorized Biography
by Amanda Bader**

razor
bill

Paul and Morgan Hamm: Olympic Heroes

RAZORBILL
Published by Penguin Group
Penguin Young Readers Group
345 Hudson Street, New York, New York 10014, U.S.A.
Penguin Books Ltd, 80 Strand, London WC2R 0RL, England
Penguin Books Australia Ltd, 250 Camberwell Road,
Camberwell, Victoria, 3124 Australia
Penguin Books Canada Ltd, 10 Alcorn Avenue, Toronto,
Ontario, Canada M4V 3B2
Penguin Books (NZ) cnr Airborne and Rosedale Roads, Albany,
Auckland 1310, New Zealand

Penguin Books Ltd, Registered Offices: Harmondsworth,
Middlesex, England

1 3 5 7 9 10 8 6 4 2

Library of Congress Cataloging-in-Publication Data is available

Printed in the United States of America

Contents

History in the Making

Twenty-year-old Paul Hamm flew through the air, holding his body straight and twisting like a corkscrew. *Just this one last move,* he reassured himself as he neared the end of his high bar routine, *and then all I have to do is stick the dismount.*

He knew he could do it this time. So did the tens of thousands of spectators packed into the Arrowhead Pond arena in Anaheim, California, to watch the 2003 World Gymnastics Championships—especially Paul's twin brother, Morgan, sitting with the rest of Team USA in the stands. Morgan was still caught up in the excitement of the victory he, Paul, and their teammates had shared earlier in the week, when together they'd captured the silver medal in the team competition. The only way to top that moment for Morgan would be to watch his brother win gold at the all-around that day.

Paul had stepped up to the high bar, the last of his six events, in second place behind China's Yang Wei, a world-class gymnast who had even won a silver medal at the Sydney Olympics in 2000. High bar wasn't always easy for Paul. In fact, in the 2001 World Championships, he had been in second place, just like today, thinking he could win it. Then, on one of his release moves, he lost his grip, his hands slipped, and he hit his face on the bar. Instead of a medal, he ended up with a bloody nose and wounded pride, falling to seventh place in the all-around standings.

Paul had used the two years that had passed since then to work on his routines and his mental toughness. High bar had always been one of his shakier events, and he knew that if he was ever going to be the best, he had to conquer it. And now all those workouts, all those hours he and Morgan had spent together in the gym, all those times he'd caught and released the bar as he worked on his routines, all of his dedication came down to this one moment.

Seconds later, when Paul's feet landed squarely on the thick, padded mat, his heart did its own special leap. He knew at that moment, before he even got his score, that he had achieved a lifelong dream—he was world champion in the men's all-around competition!

The audience, watching his routine in awed silence, erupted with cheers of support. But no one cheered harder than Morgan. Winning a team medal side by side had been fantastic, but now Paul had taken the twins even further—he'd made history, becoming the first American man to win a gold medal in the all-around competition of the World Gymnastics Championships!

No matter what happened in the rest of his career, Paul Hamm would always be listed in the record books as the 2003 world champion. "It feels incredible," he said.

But the fact was, it was just one more incredible moment on top of many that the extraordinary gymnast had already experienced. And the best part, for Paul, was being able to share it once more with his twin, Morgan. Because no matter which one stands on the medals podium, Paul and Morgan each credit the other with making them the gymnasts they are today.

CHAPTER ONE

The Early Years

If you ask the Hamm twins how they discovered their love of gymnastics, they'll say it's their sister, Betsy's, fault.

Huh?

Most gymnasts are chock-full of stories about how their parents finally enrolled them in a program at a local gym so they would stop jumping on the furniture and bouncing off the walls. Even the ones who have become international stars still remember how much they loved the chance to climb, tumble, swing, and jump without getting yelled at for making a mess in the house.

But that's not how it happened for

Paul and Morgan Hamm.

Morgan and Paul were born on September 24, 1982, in Waukesha, Wisconsin, a medium-size city near Milwaukee. Their mother, Cecily, had grown up in Glen Ellyn, Illinois, and had settled with her husband, Sandy, in Wisconsin shortly after she got out of college. Their first child, Betsy, was born in June 1980. Betsy was still a toddler when the Hamms went to the hospital to give birth to their second child. They told Betsy they'd be bringing home a surprise—a new sibling—but it turned out the Hamms were the ones in for a shock!

Moments after Cecily gave birth to a baby boy, doctors broke some incredible news that somehow no one had seen earlier—there was another baby coming. An hour later, the Hamms had a totally unexpected set of twin boys!

Cecily and Sandy had planned to name their son Morgan Paul Hamm, so they had to think fast when it turned out they needed more names. In the end, they called the "older" baby Morgan Ebert—after Cecily's dad—and gave Paul his dad's middle name, Carl, so he's Paul Carl Hamm.

Growing up, Paul and Morgan were certainly full of energy, but they weren't exactly knocking into sofas like most future gymnastics stars. The twins were way too busy trying lots of different hobbies—soccer, T-ball, even piano lessons. Then in 1989, seven-year-old Paul noticed all the jumping, twisting, and spinning his older sister, Betsy, was doing for her gymnastics lessons. It looked like a lot of fun, and he asked his mother if he could try gymnastics. Cecily didn't see why not, so she signed Paul up for his first class.

Little did his mother know that Paul's desire to be like his big sister would change the Hamm family's life forever.

Cecily started out by enrolling Paul in

a twelve-week class to give him a chance to see if he liked the sport as much as he thought he would. Watching the kids practice, she was overwhelmed by how many different moves there were to learn. Gymnastics clearly required a lot of strength as well as balance. As Cecily gaped at the more-experienced students working on their back handsprings, splits, and flips, she never imagined that any of her kids would reach that level. But right from the start, Paul was a natural. He was able to learn tricks and tumbling moves much faster than the other kids, and it seemed like he couldn't get enough of it. In fact, Paul was learning so much faster than anyone else in his class that he got bored after just a month. His mom was puzzled when he told her he didn't want go to class anymore. She asked him why not, when he seemed to love the sport so much. Paul explained it wasn't that he didn't like gymnastics—he loved it! He just got tired of waiting around for the other kids to figure out how to do the things that he could get in one try. He begged his parents to find him a tougher class, one that would really challenge him.

Wow—it looked like this latest hobby was turning out to be more serious than Paul's parents had expected! Not only that, but Cecily and Sandy soon had two sons asking for gymnastics lessons. "Big" brother Morgan didn't want to miss out on anything. If Betsy and Paul were having so much fun, Morgan wanted to make sure he got to take lessons as well.

When the Hamms realized just how excited their kids were about gymnastics, Sandy got to work setting up a makeshift gym in the backyard so they could practice. It was nothing fancy—the high bar was made of steel, old stairway rails served as parallel bars, and the "pommel horse" was actually a leather-covered tree trunk—but the boys still spent hours and hours working on their skills. As he watched his sons learn tricks on the homemade equipment, Sandy could see how talented they were—and how much they enjoyed it!

Sandy had been an All-American diver when he was in college, so he knew how important good coaching was in creating a top-level athlete. When it became clear that the boys' natural ability and desire was something special—even beyond what their sister, Betsy, who had been their inspiration, was capable of—Sandy realized he needed to hire a private coach to work with his sons.

A neighbor told Sandy about a man named Stacy Maloney, who was offering lessons in a Milwaukee gym not far from the Hamms' home. Maloney was a former gymnast who had competed in college and had even been a member of the U.S. Men's Senior National Team before turning to coaching. Sandy immediately learned all he could about Maloney. After watching him in the movie *American Anthem*, where Maloney shows his stuff alongside famous Olympic gymnast Mitch Gaylord, Sandy Hamm made up his mind—this was the man to coach his boys.

There was just one problem. While it was true that Maloney was giving some lessons in Milwaukee, his heart really wasn't in gymnastics anymore. Since moving back to Wisconsin, Stacy had started a band that played in local clubs, and he was even trying to get a recording contract. He really wanted to focus on music, so he wasn't interested in taking on the demanding schedule of private lessons for two kids who wanted to immerse themselves entirely in gymnastics.

For Sandy, taking no for an answer wasn't really an option. He kept after Stacy and finally wore him down. Couldn't Maloney at least come take a *look* at his sons? Reluctantly, Stacy finally agreed to come and see what Paul and Morgan could do.

It turned out to be almost as much fun for Stacy as it was for the boys. He quickly realized that the twins were not only physically talented; they were good listeners and quick learners. He'd explain a trick to them and they'd have it on the next try. He remembers, "I recognized right from the beginning that [Paul and Morgan] had the physical and mental combination, the whole package." Stacy Maloney believed the Hamm boys could make it on the international gymnastics scene. Even at that early stage, the thought of the Olympics came into his mind.

Suddenly Stacy's music career became a thing of the past, almost overnight. He knew that the chance to coach athletes like Paul and Morgan was a once-in-a-lifetime thing. He was happy to find himself devoting more and more time to helping Paul and Morgan explore their potential as national- and hopefully international-level gymnasts.

With older sister Betsy improving rapidly (even though not quite on the level of Paul and Morgan) and the twins learning so quickly, the Hamms decided they really needed to find a gym for everyone. They picked Swiss Turners, a gymnastics academy that had a long history of success.

At Swiss Turners, the atmosphere was completely alive with gymnastics and exactly what all of the Hamms had been looking for. The twins took to it like fish to water! They were surrounded by other dedicated athletes, which was the best motivation for them to learn faster.

Although Betsy wasn't as serious as her brothers, she was still improving all the time and earned a spot on the U.S. Senior team at the end of high school. She was recruited for college by the

University of Florida and had an awesome freshman year, winning first place on the balance beam event at the NCAA (college) Championships. In that meet she was also fourth in the all-around, earning the best score of any freshman at the meet.

Betsy never did reach as far as her brothers, but she was still happy with her own accomplishments and thrilled to watch Paul and Morgan compete. "When I was little, Paul used to teach me stuff. He was always the bravest of the three of us," Betsy remembers. Was Betsy jealous of the potential everyone—including herself—saw in her brothers? Nope, she was as proud as could be. And she could always take credit for being the first one to get them interested in gymnastics!

It was something Betsy would grow even more proud of as it became clear that major gymnastic success was in store for Paul and Morgan Hamm.

CHAPTER TWO

Hitting the Big Time

Stacy Maloney had worked out with some of the best American gymnasts of his time both in college and during the production of *American Anthem*. But he had never seen anything like what he observed with the Hamm twins—he just couldn't get over how quickly they were able to learn new skills.

While most fourteen-year old boys are busy with school and friends, Paul and Morgan spent more than twenty hours a week in the gym. School and homework just had to be fitted in somehow while they moved up the ranks of boys' gymnastics. Along with their teammates from

Swiss Turners, Morgan and Paul competed in local and regional club meets as well as the state and regional finals.

The Hamms were successful enough that in 1996 they both competed in their first Junior Olympic Nationals—a nationwide meet that brings together the best young gymnasts in the country. It was a great chance for them to see how they compared to other boys, and the answer was a good one: Paul was second overall and Morgan was thirteenth. That meant they got to go to national team training camps, where they worked on their skills with Coach Maloney and with other coaches and competitors from around the country. Next, Paul got to be on board for the 1996 Junior Pan American Games, helping America win the bronze medal behind Cuba and Canada!

Big junior meets were one thing, but the twins got their first real look at the "big time" (and experienced their first big-time jitters!) when the tremendously popular Tour of World Gymnastics Champions came to Milwaukee after the 1996 Olympics in Atlanta.

American success at the Olympic Games had created intense interest in gymnastics. The women's team—nicknamed the Magnificent Seven—had captured the country's heart when they unexpectedly won a team gold medal. Though the men's team finished out of the medals in fifth place, it seemed like everyone who had ever watched gymnastics was interested in seeing the Olympic stars on their triumphant national tour. All around the country gymnastics clubs, teams, and fans bought blocks of tickets to the shows so they could watch and cheer as their new heroes performed their routines in this exhibition. Of course when the tour came to Milwaukee, the Swiss Turners were there in full force.

For added excitement in each city, some

of the better young gymnasts from each town got to perform with the Olympians. Guess who got to go from the Swiss Turners club? Yep—Paul and Morgan Hamm.

Even at age fourteen, they had already competed in big meets, but this was different. Morgan confessed, "We were a little nervous. We've performed in front of big crowds before, but not this big." After all, there were almost 20,000 enthusiastic fans packing Milwaukee's Bradley Center to enjoy the show.

Despite the huge crowd that focused their attention on Paul during his thirty-second high bar routine, Paul nailed his routine perfectly and stuck the dismount like a pro. The hometown fans cheered so loudly, you would have thought Paul had won a medal! At that moment, he and Morgan knew that this was what they wanted to do. Not only was doing gymnastics a total blast, it was pretty fun to please the crowds, too.

Seeing how well Paul and Morgan had performed while surrounded by Olympians and in front of the big crowd affirmed what Coach Maloney had believed all along—the boys should set their sights on going to the Olympics.

The twins thought it sounded a little far-fetched but . . . why not? The year 2000 sounded so far away, anything could happen. Paul remembers, "We decided then that we were just going to shoot for it and see how close we got."

Coach Maloney explained that the road to Australia meant the twins would have to spend more time training, and they would also would need to find ways to balance out their lack of international competitive experience.

Under Maloney's guidance, Paul and Morgan learned there was more to gymnastics than just picking up tricks and putting them together in routines. Coach believed that one way they could be better than the kids they competed against was to really study the sport. He taught them to apply themselves to learning all about gymnastics the same way they studied a subject in school.

Participating in big meets that were held in different parts of the country was also part of their education. Being away from home, in different cities, surrounded by kids they didn't know that well wasn't easy. But Maloney knew it was important to get Paul and Morgan comfortable with traveling and performing well on the road so the twins would be able to focus regardless of the surroundings.

In 1998, Paul was again chosen to be a member of the U.S. team at the Junior Pan American Games. The U.S. team beat twenty-two other nations to win the gold medal, and Paul won an individual bronze medal on parallel bars. "It's great to win this year," Paul said, thinking back to the team bronze he'd come away with in 1996.

The winning didn't stop there—Paul's strong routines were also a key part of the gold medal won by the Junior Men's team at the International Team Championships in Knoxville, Tennessee.

The twins were starting to get used to bigger competitions, but they still got a major case of nerves before the 1998 John Hancock U.S. Gymnastics Championships held in Indianapolis, Indiana, where the U.S. national champion would be crowned. Paul and Morgan were competing in a division with other fourteen- and fifteen-year-olds, so they weren't in contention for the top prize. Still, they'd be out there warming up and taking the floor alongside their idols, the best gymnasts in the country! Guys like twenty-four-year-old Blaine Wilson, who had two national championships under his belt already and had been to the 1996 Olympics in Atlanta.

As nerve-racking as it was to be

surrounded by the best of the best, the Hamms nailed their own routines like they had been at it for a lifetime. Paul won first place in the all-around, tied for the individual gold medal in rings, and had three other silver medal finishes. "My international competition experience really helped me to concentrate on hitting all of my routines," Paul explained. Morgan was fourth in the all-around, tied his brother Paul for a silver medal on floor exercise, and won the pommel horse title. And when their scores were considered against the scores of gymnasts who *were* competing in the Senior Men's division, Paul would have finished thirtieth and Morgan thirty-fifth overall. Not bad at all! As a result of their success, they were both named to the U.S. Junior Nationals team again.

The year 1999 found the twins' winning ways continuing. They both had super results at the Junior Olympic National Championships in Houston, Texas, with

Paul tying for first and Morgan winning third in the all-around.

It was clear that the boys, who were already extraordinary, were improving at a rapid pace. How did they do it? "A big part of it is getting stronger," Paul explained. At the age of sixteen, the twins were about five feet, six inches tall and weighed somewhere around 135 pounds . . . of solid muscle. Though female gymnasts are very strong, they're almost always petite and reach their athletic peak in their mid-teens. Male gymnasts need strength to perform the amazing feats they do, which is part of why the top men's gymnasts are usually in their twenties. But all those grueling workouts were paying off for the Hamms because they seemed to be ahead of the curve!

In fact, when Paul and Morgan returned to the John Hancock U.S. Gymnastics Championships in 1999, they were both there to compete against the senior men.

If they could rank high enough in the event, they'd be bumped up to the next level and join the U.S. Men's Senior squad!

Paul soon proved he was up to the task when he finished eleventh in the men's competition, earning one of fourteen spots on the Men's Senior National Team. Paul's berth on the team meant that he would go and train at national camps right alongside national champion Blaine Wilson, gymnastics great John Roethlisberger, and the rest of the top gymnasts in the country.

Morgan had a strong meet, capturing the Junior Elite division for his age group, but he missed the Senior team by just two places, finishing sixteenth. Uh-oh—that meant that for the first time ever, the twins would be split up, with Paul on the Senior squad and Morgan still on the Junior team. The twins were *not* happy with that. They had to find a way to get Morgan back alongside Paul, and fast!

CHAPTER THREE

Sibling Revelry

Paul and Morgan were sure of one thing—they had to get Morgan up on the U.S. Senior team soon if he and Paul were going to fulfill their goal of making it to the 2000 Olympics together. All they needed was a chance to prove Morgan could hold his own.

That opportunity came at the 2000 Winter Cup, held every February in Las Vegas, Nevada. Open to the top 100 male gymnasts in the United States, the Winter Cup is the first serious meet of the season. Paul had been at the 1999 Winter Cup Challenge, finishing a respectable twenty-first in the all-around, and he and

Morgan headed there together in 2000.

There was already buzz about Paul in Las Vegas. Coaches and competitors had noticed how quickly he was maturing, how consistently he performed, and how well he kept his focus under pressure. But Morgan was determined to prove that he was cut from the same tough cloth as his brother.

The boys had a good preliminary round, turning in strong, consistent routines and earning good scores. Paul was in third for the all-around after the preliminary round, and Morgan was in twelfth. The object was for Morgan to finish in the top ten so he would make the Senior team and really be in contention for the Olympic Trials. And he sure didn't want to miss it by two places again, like he had at the U.S. Championships. So twelfth was okay, but it wasn't going to be good enough.

The good news was that Morgan felt very confident.

In the finals, when he stood and saluted the judges before starting his floor exercise, he realized just how self-assured he felt. He took a deep breath, then launched into his first tumbling run and didn't stop hitting skills until the routine was over and he had stuck the dismount. Grinning, he threw his hands up in response to the crowd's applause as he left the podium. He knew he had nailed the whole thing, and the judges thought so, too—they gave him a 9.80! His other strongest event was the vault, and he didn't disappoint. He hit a powerful and stylish vault to place second, taking the silver.

As they went through the rotations to each event, Morgan felt more and more sure of himself; he knew he was having a good meet. He was hitting his routines consistently, doing what he needed to do to gain two positions between the preliminaries and the final rounds. The twins both acknowledge that Paul pushes harder in the gym—Morgan says Paul is "sometimes pretty bossy" about their workouts. But in the arena in Las Vegas, Morgan realized that all the extra work Paul had made him do was paying off.

Coach Maloney talked to Morgan between events, encouraging him to keep his focus, remain calm, and even visualize himself nailing the new routines they had practiced.

After four events, Paul was in eighth and Morgan was in ninth; they had only the vault and the parallel bars left. Morgan was strong in the vault but often struggled with the parallel bars. The boys both wanted Morgan to make the top ten so badly, Coach thought they might be getting distracted. He had a plan: Since Paul's spot on the national team was already assured, what if Paul didn't do his parallel bars routine? That would help Morgan's chances of keeping his top-ten position, wouldn't it? Of course it would! It was a good plan and they decided to go with it. So in the last rotation, Paul did exactly what he needed to do to help his brother: he sat out his last event to remove any chance of beating Morgan.

Wow—talk about brotherly love! It was an amazing sacrifice, showing how Morgan's success truly meant as much to Paul as his own.

In fact, on the sidelines, Paul was more nervous watching Morgan compete than he had been at any other point in the meet! Sitting and watching Morgan do his parallel bars routine, Paul realized he couldn't imagine what it would be like to go to important meets without Morgan. The minute Morgan landed his dismount, Paul and Coach Maloney knew that their plan had worked. Morgan finished sixth, and the brothers were reunited on the U.S. Senior team.

Sandy and Cecily couldn't have been prouder of their sons, but not just because of Paul and Morgan's outstanding performances in the meet. What made them happiest was seeing how the twins were able to share their success so easily, without any jealousy or rivalry.

In fact, the boys have always been extremely close. "We're best friends. We have a great relationship," Morgan says.

But how do brothers who care so much about the same thing spend all that time together and not drive each other crazy? Well, there *are* plenty of differences between the twins. They certainly look alike, of course—the same strawberry blond hair, a light dose of freckles, and *lots* of muscles, especially in their shoulders and arms. They have high foreheads and strong chins and both have friendly smiles. Coach Maloney can tell who's who out in the gym, but when the twins go to training camps or on tour, the coaches who haven't worked with them all their lives say they have to check in the morning to see who's wearing what color T-shirt because once they get out on the gym floor, it can be tough to tell them apart.

But those who pay close attention know there are a bunch of ways they're different. For one thing, Morgan's a lefty and Paul's a righty. You can see it when they're doing gymnastics—Morgan does his round-offs to the right and Paul does them to the left. Plus their noses are different shapes, their smiles aren't identical, and their hair's a little different, too. Morgan's hair stays parted in the middle, while Paul's drifts together a bit.

Their family and teammates who spend time with them know that there are differences in their personalities, too. Morgan tends to be more outgoing and relaxed. Usually he's the one cracking the jokes and chatting with strangers, though Paul has gotten much better at small talk as he's spent more time touring and competing.

Sometimes Paul is quiet because he's

shy, and sometimes it's a result of his general intensity. In the gym, both twins agree Paul's the one who's always pushing the training harder, doing one more routine, making sure he lets Morgan know if there's more work to be done. Morgan jokes that he compensates for all the gymnastics-related bossiness by being the one who is more dominant when they're not in the gym.

They lived in separate rooms at home (it was too much togetherness for Paul when they shared a room) and took separate classes at school, only getting together to drive thirty minutes each way to their practices twice a day.

They were apart enough in high school that, before they started getting lots of coverage in the local newspaper sports section, many students at Waukesha South didn't know there were two of them. Cecily tells a story of one confused student who kept asking Paul what the

Spanish homework was without realizing he was talking to the twin who was taking German!

Morgan tends to have slightly better grades than Paul, although they're pretty much even. They were both honors students, even though being on the road during gymnastics season means they missed close to three weeks of classes in high school.

They freely acknowledge that Paul is the more driven of the two and that it helps both of them in the gym. It could be that extra bit of dedication is what helped Paul become a little stronger all-around. But Morgan has his own specialties. He actually has stronger legs, so he excels in the vault and in floor exercises, while Paul's upper-body strength pushes him ahead in parallel bars, pommel horse, high bar, and rings. Paul catches on to things a little bit faster, but Morgan keeps at it until he learns it.

They are both very focused on being the best they can; Paul just seems to push himself and his brother harder, while Morgan is always there to support his brother, and his more relaxed attitude toward life can help Paul stay cool.

Coach Maloney credits the Hamm parents with giving the boys a healthy perspective on gymnastics. "We always try to walk the line between being supportive and being pushy," Cecily explains. "It's what they want to do." The twins knew they had the option to quit—they didn't need to do gymnastics to get their parents' attention or love. As Cecily puts it, "It's just gymnastics; it's not earth-shattering."

That might be Cecily's opinion, but no matter what she told her sons, gymnastics was still everything to Paul and Morgan. Now that they'd both made it to the U.S. Men's Senior team, they had just one goal left—competing at the upcoming 2000 Olympics.

CHAPTER FOUR

International Hopes

Once Morgan had secured his spot on the Senior team, Coach Maloney warned him that it was time to make some of his routines harder so that he'd have a chance at the highest scores possible.

Every skill a gymnast does is rated for difficulty by the International Gymnastics Federation (called the FIG for short). When a routine is created, the values of the skills in that routine are added up to make the start value, which is the best-possible score a gymnast can get if he does his routine perfectly. The most difficult routine is valued at 10—that's called a start value of 10. Easier routines have lower start values.

As each gymnast performs, the judges deduct points for mistakes. So if two-tenths of a point are deducted from a routine with a start value of 10, the final score is 9.8. But if the routine wasn't that hard to begin with, it might only have a start value of 9.5, so losing the same two-tenths of a point would yield a score of 9.3.

Coach Maloney knew that if his pupils wanted to have a chance of making it to the Olympics to compete against the best gymnasts in the world, they needed start values of 10.0 on every event. This was already true for Paul's routines, so Coach Maloney just had to work on increasing the difficulty on Morgan's vault and high bar routines.

In July they took those new routines to the GymJam Nationals, held in Santa Barbara, California. GymJam was actually a qualifier for the John Hancock U.S. Gymnastics Championships, but since Paul and Morgan had pre-qualified for the U.S. nationals based on their previous success, they treated the meet as an opportunity to practice their more difficult routines in a competition setting without too much at stake.

GymJam was another successful meet for the boys, with Paul finishing third behind Blaine Wilson and John Roethlisberger (you don't get much closer than *that* to the big guys!) and Morgan garnering fifth. Coach Maloney was pleased that the two of them were gaining confidence daily; all part of the plan.

The twins had one more hurdle to get to the Olympic Trials in August: the good old John Hancock U.S. Gymnastics Championships, held in St. Louis, Missouri. They had to be among the top fourteen finishers at these U.S. nationals to earn a chance to try out for the Olympic team. Ultimately, team selections would be made based on the U.S. National Gymnastics Championship scores and the athlete's performance at the Olympic Trials.

The atmosphere was charged in St. Louis's Kiel Center. Every athlete there had Olympic dreams. Paul and Morgan performed well in the preliminary round, staying focused, managing their nerves, and watching the other competitors.

They were getting used to competing against incredible athletes like Blaine Wilson, John Roethlisberger, Sean Townsend (an experienced young gymnast who had been part of the 1999 World Championship team), and up-and-coming Guard Young, whose father was a gymnast who had been NCAA champion and had gone to the 1976 Olympics. And as they got more comfortable, the boys knew it was important to watch these gymnasts and learn from them. After all, it's not every day you get to see someone get a 9.950 on the still rings, and that's just what Blaine did at the U.S. Championships!

Coach Maloney made sure the twins took the opportunity to pay attention to the ways these guys handled pressure and what they did when they made mistakes and to observe their techniques firsthand.

The top athletes were watching the Hamms, too. Guys like John Roethlisberger, who was considered the leader of the U.S. team, wanted to be sure that American gymnasts continued to do well in international competition. When the U.S. team went to meets together, everyone helped everyone else because it was important for them to do well—not just as individuals, but as a team, too. So there was a tradition of the older guys looking out for the younger guys. After a particularly tough time at the U.S. Championships, John Roethlisberger was asked by a reporter what he thought about the Hamm twins. He shook his head and answered, "All I can say is that I'm glad I'm retiring after this year. These guys are setting the standard for the younger gymnasts. Future generations are going to have to match up to them." That was high praise from someone who knew and cared about the future of gymnastics.

After the preliminary round, Paul was fourth and Morgan was tenth. Since the top fourteen would go on to the Olympic Trials, they were in good positions as long as they did well in the finals, but Paul had made it clear that he wanted to finish in the top four.

To keep his fourth place through the finals, Paul was going to have to lay down some pretty awesome routines. And that's what he set out to do. While Paul was powering through his routines, he was (as usual) pushing Morgan to do the same . . . and it was working! Morgan proved that he was strong on each of the events, even garnering the best floor exercise score of the meet, a 9.70.

Going into the last rotation, vault, the

twins' places were pretty well assured, but they still had a chance to improve. Morgan was up first. He stood on the podium and saluted, took a deep breath, and accelerated down the approach, completely focused on the vaulting table. He absolutely attacked his vault, getting great height and sticking the landing, as he had so many times in practice! Paul jumped off his chair and ran over to congratulate his brother with their usual high ten.

When it came time for his own vault, he must have been trying too hard. The height was good, but he missed sticking the landing and "sat down" (gymnasts' expression for a fall that leaves you sitting) on the mat. Despite his mistake, he still got a respectable 9.30, which was good enough for sixth place on the vault.

Steve McCain—a three-time World team member who had even founded the Web site AmericanGymnast—was in third place ahead of Paul. But he soon blew his pommel horse routine and ended up with an 8.850, which was definitely going to hurt his standings.

Even before the official results were announced, the twins were all smiles, celebrating with Coach Maloney. They didn't need all those numbers to know that they had done exactly what they had set out to do—get to the Olympic Trials.

Despite the bobble on vault, Paul's strong performances in the other events added up to a third-place finish. He had exceeded his goal of fourth place and had even won a medal! Morgan's finals round was fourth best, and when it was combined with his tenth-place preliminary score, he had finished in eighth place overall. He would be going to the Olympic Trials right next to his brother, Paul, just as they had planned!

CHAPTER FIVE

Olympic Selection Trials

Any celebration the Hamms had after the U.S. Championships was short and sweet. With only three weeks in between meets, there was simply no time to relax.

It was no secret that Paul was the stronger overall competitor of the two. What if he made the Olympic team and Morgan didn't? What would that do to Morgan? And Paul was so used to having his brother's support—could he make it through the Olympics on his own?

When the twins were asked what

would happen if they weren't both selected for the Olympics, they always responded that if one didn't make it, he'd still be happy for the one who did. As Morgan put it, no matter what, it would just be great to have a brother who went to the Olympics. "How many people can actually say that?" he said, always the easygoing soul, adding, "We'd both still have another shot in 2004."

The best thing the boys could do was practice, focus, and think positively. They kept up their usual twice-a-day workouts and concentrated their thoughts on both making the team. They went to classes, but it certainly was hard to pay attention to learning history when the pair were trying to make it by being the first twins to become Olympic gymnasts!

Three weeks, which had seemed like such a short time to prepare for such an important event, ended up feeling like an eternity. All of this waiting around and talking was much harder than doing gymnastics. The boys just wanted to get to Boston and show what they could do! Finally the time came, and the whole family headed east.

Although this was the most important meet the boys had ever been in, it was the smallest in sheer numbers. They were only competing against fifteen other gymnasts—but, of course, fifteen pretty *amazing* gymnasts!

Out of these fifteen, six guys would go to Sydney. The choices would be made based on a combination of scores from the U.S. Championships and the Olympic Trials (the scores from Boston would count a little more than the ones from St. Louis). The first four finishers were assured of an Olympic berth. The last two spots would be chosen by a special committee, which would consider the gymnasts' performance in the meets and the special strengths the athletes had demonstrated in a particular event.

So while Paul was coming into Boston

in third place, a strong position, Morgan's spot on the team was much less certain. He knew his solid performances on the floor exercise, vault, and rings might be important to the selection committee, but he still had to improve his standing overall to be considered.

The whole atmosphere felt different from a normal meet—fewer people but *way* more attention. Everywhere the twins went, there were journalists, and it seemed like every one of them wanted to talk to the Hamms.

In fact, because hopes were high for the United States in Sydney, the trials were going to be broadcast live on television. There were guys with cameras everywhere, walking right up to the athletes and practically sticking the lenses in their faces. It didn't matter what the gymnasts were doing—changing uniforms, chalking their hands—there was a camera, recording every move!

Pressure? Oh, not *too* much!

But according to everyone who saw them, the twins just didn't seem intimidated by all of the hoopla that was going on around them. Peter Kormann, the U.S. men's Olympic coach, called the twins amazing, saying, "You get a certain feeling, just watching them, that they don't get their cage rattled like some of the younger guys. It's a special quality."

At least once the preliminaries got started on Thursday evening, Paul and Morgan could focus on their events.

They started out on parallel bars, where Paul tried to concentrate on his own routine, which had been strong, rather than think about the fact that Morgan had bobbled one of his moves. They moved on to high bar, where Morgan cheered along with the rest of the crowd when Paul got a 9.75 for a smooth, clean routine.

It was clear that Paul was "in the

zone"—performing at his best. He was having a great meet. Both brothers really nailed their floor exercise routines, and they were thrilled when the scores were posted and Morgan had even beaten Paul, earning the best score of everyone on the floor, a 9.825.

That hopeful excitement turned to disappointment when Morgan fell off the pommel horse early in his routine. He shook his head and got right back on, repeating the sequence and completing his routine, but it wasn't a strong one. Paul was right there, as always, to motivate Morgan and get him back on track. They tried not to pay attention to the disappointment of his 8.50 and to look ahead to the rest of the events.

Just the rings and vault to go, and both boys executed all of their skills well. They high-tenned and hugged as they saw the preliminary round scores: Paul was in an unbelievable second place! The only gymnast who had beaten him was the amazing Blaine Wilson. If Paul could keep this up, his trip to the Olympics was assured.

Morgan, who had been a very strong fourth in the preliminary rounds, was still in sixth overall, despite his problems on pommel horse. That left his chances as uncertain as ever. But Paul, trying to keep him psyched for the finals, pointed out that Morgan had posted the best floor score and his rings and vault had both been strong. Coach Maloney agreed, saying that it was likely the selection committee would want Morgan's skills on floor, vault, and maybe even rings to round out the team based on the weaknesses of the four guys who had already qualified.

Though everyone thought he looked calm, Morgan had actually been much more nervous than he had expected. Having done pretty well in the first round, he promised himself, his brother, and his coach that he would be calmer and more prepared for the finals on Saturday.

When the media asked him about his brother's success, Morgan simply said that he found it very helpful to have his brother there to push him through the competition. Neither brother wanted to think about the possibility of one of them making the team and the other being left behind. They were in this together. As Coach Maloney put it, "It's more like those two versus everyone else."

Finals day turned out to be longer and more stressful than either Morgan or Paul ever expected. Unless Paul had a disaster, he was assured a spot at the Olympics. Paul was managing his competition nerves okay, but watching Morgan was really hard for him. Used to bossing his brother around, Paul just looked Morgan in the eye and told him he wanted to see him hitting his routines. Period. Morgan must have listened because he did a fine job.

The twins made it through all of their routines without any serious flaws; Morgan even tied Blaine Wilson for the best score on the floor exercise. He later said that he was so nervous on his last event, pommel horse, that his knees were shaking. It was hard to get over the intimidation of knowing he'd messed up on the apparatus before, but he just kept pulling his mind back to his routine and somehow got through it.

When all of the rotations were done, four athletes, including Paul, Blaine, Sean Townsend, and Steve McCain knew for sure that they were going to Sydney. Then the hard part came: All the athletes had to wait in the same room for more than half an hour while the selection committee debated who would fill the last two spots.

Morgan sat in that locker room with his head in his hands, trying not to think about the possibility of Paul going to the Olympics without him. He kept going over and over the results, trying to figure out what was going to happen. Ahead of Morgan in fifth place was Jamie Natalie, who had scored two 9.625s and an awesome 9.9 on high bar. Behind Morgan in seventh was John Roethlisberger. That was scary because John would surely get extra consideration from the committee since he was at the end of a long and successful career; he was a proven competitor, despite having had a bad meet.

Some of the gymnasts snacked and chatted, but Paul could see that Morgan was really scared. He sat next to him and just talked quietly, trying to keep him calm. It was hard to cut through the tension in the room.

Had they ever been so nervous? Probably not.

Finally, after what seemed like hours, they were called back out to the floor. They wouldn't know who had made the team until the announcement was made in front of the crowd. And it was going to be made in alphabetical order. Quickly going over everyone's names, Morgan realized he'd know after the first name whether he was going with his brother or not.

Gulp.

It was a long walk out to the floor, and the crowd fell silent as the announcer asked for their attention. Morgan held his breath. The first name called was Jamie Natalie's . . . as an alternate. Morgan exhaled and looked at Paul, trying not to smile before he knew for sure but . . . then the announcer said his name. Morgan was stunned and then thrilled. He thought he was going to burst! He tried hard to stay composed as the announcer named the rest of the team; the last wild-card spot had gone to

John Roethlisberger, who cried when he found out he would get a third chance at an Olympic medal.

Incredibly, the committee had decided they could count on Morgan's strength in the floor exercise and vault. Morgan and Paul were ecstatic. And in the stands, the rest of their family was going wild! All of their worries about what to do if only one made the team were gone. Plus they had a nifty little bonus that most Olympic athletes don't get. Each athlete can usually bring only one parent along, but since Paul and Morgan were both going to the Olympics, that meant both Sandy and Cecily would get to go to Australia as well!

When Paul and Morgan got home, they found they were media stars, not just in Wisconsin but all over the country. After all, they were the only twins *ever* selected for a men's Olympic gymnastics team, and it seemed like everyone wanted to know how they felt. Well, they felt like they were walking on air. As Paul put it, the Olympics were a dream; the Olympics with each other was the best dream they had ever had.

After years of working with Coach Maloney and competing for Swiss Turners, Paul and Morgan now had a bunch of new teammates (only the best in the country!) and would be heading out to San Diego to train with the team and the Olympic coaches.

Wow—they'd been so focused on making the team, but now the reality was starting to sink in. The Olympics started in less than a month, and they had so much preparation to do. They were about to represent their country in the biggest gymnastics competition in the world!

CHAPTER SIX

An Olympic First

What's the best excuse—*ever*—for missing class? How about making history as the first set of twins to ever compete in the same Olympic event? Paul and Morgan had to miss the whole first month of their senior year to travel to Sydney for the Olympic Games.

But the twins didn't get off that easy—they still had homework assignments with them that they were supposed to do in Australia. Somehow they were going to have to juggle their schoolwork with the most exciting competition of their lives!

Although the twins had traveled a bit

already, Sydney, a beautiful city with modern architecture on a huge harbor, was unlike anyplace they had been before. Aside from being halfway around the world, the Hamms found that just being at the Olympic Village was awesome. In the village, there were hundreds of athletes from around the world, speaking all kinds of different languages. Morgan was thrilled to see Luc Longley, a basketball player who had played for the Chicago Bulls. The twins also met Olympic decathlon gold medalist Dan O'Brien, and Paul even had his photo taken with The Greatest, Muhammad Ali.

In the month since the Olympic Trials, the American gymnastics team had trained intensely together and had really bonded into a unit. Despite the age differences, the team really got along well and there was a lot of mutual respect. The older guys, who had been to lots of international competitions, teased the

Hamm twins that they were like sponges, trying to absorb everything they saw. And who wouldn't want to remember their first Olympic experience?

John, the team captain, gave Paul and Morgan some very useful advice. He told them five points to keep in mind as they practiced and competed. They were "Never give up," "Stay in control," "Fight for every tenth [of a point in the score]," "Stick your dismounts," and "Be proud of yourself and your team." Those would prove to be important things to remember as the Olympics went on.

When the team walked into the huge Olympic Park arena for the first workout on Wednesday, September 13, the sight of the place, draped with flags from every country and already filling up with spectators, just took Morgan's breath away.

Once they got down to business, though, the team quickly discovered that there were some technical issues. Mainly that the surface for the floor exercise was so bouncy, it was like a trampoline, according to Coach Kormann. They did lots of tumbling runs to try to get used to the extra springiness, but the guys kept over-rotating and missing their moves, not a good way to settle anyone's nerves before a big competition.

Paul and Morgan weren't the only American gymnasts to feel lumps in their throats as they walked into the Olympic Park arena for the start of the competition on September 16. There were over 100 men, each the best in his country and some the best in the world, all vying for Olympic glory.

Sean said he was so overwhelmed by the honor of representing his country that he had to fight back tears more than once. Paul couldn't get over the energy in the packed arena; the air was positively electric. Walking out onto the floor in his U.S. Olympic team attire was the most amazing experience of his life. More than once, he and Morgan looked at each other in disbelief—was it really them? Were they really there? Awesome!

If the boys were nervous when they woke up on that first day of their first Olympic competition, they got even edgier when John dislocated his index finger during the warm-up session for the team qualifying. Would he be able to compete? Even with the injury, the other team-mates would still have a chance, but they'd be losing John from the events that he was best at.

Team meets often have different rules about how many team members compete and are scored. There were six men in Sydney ready to compete for the American team, but only five (named by Coach Kormann) actually competed in each event, so that some gymnasts sat out certain events. The best four scores of the five who competed would count toward the team all-around final, so that gymnasts who were good enough to compete in more events would end up competing at the all-around. Paul, Blaine, and Steve were competing in all six events, giving them the best chance of qualifying. Morgan, however, wasn't supposed to compete on the parallel bars and high bar, his weaker events. Everything changed when John realized that he wasn't going to be able to compete on the parallel bars. At the last minute, Morgan found out that he was going to have to take John's place. As if he needed more pressure!

The beginning of the first rotation was rough on Team USA. Paul, Sean, Steve, and Blaine all had trouble on the floor exercise. The floor was so springy, they all had a hard time managing a landing or two; each of them stepped out-of-bounds, a rare mistake for gymnasts at their level. Morgan, feeling the pressure of *having* to perform perfectly as he watched the mistakes, was the only one who nailed his routine just fine, hitting his skills and landing his double-layout dismount as though he had done it forever. He scored a very respectable 9.612 and got an enthusiastic high five from Coach Kormann.

Mistakes continued to dog the team through the next two rotations. The gymnasts just weren't in their zones. John kept reminding them of the five points, and finally, on vault, things started to come together.

Paul tried to force himself to ignore the image of the three German team members who had gone right before him and lost their balance badly on their vault landings. That was only making him more nervous. The other guys kept telling him he could do it, and he knew he needed to believe them. When it was his turn, he put all doubts out of his mind, accelerated toward the vaulting table, and . . . absolutely nailed his most difficult vault. Wow—he couldn't believe he'd stuck it! And in the most important competition of his life. He was relieved and elated all at the same time.

Grinning from ear to ear, he returned to the bench to cheer his teammates on. Morgan took his cue from Paul, stepped up to the podium, raised his hand to salute the judges, and pounded down the approach to land his vault, too. Now Paul was doubly proud. Then Sean stuck *his* landing for a 9.650 and they were on a roll.

When Blaine went on to stick his vault, too, the whole team jumped up to congratulate him. *Finally,* Paul thought, *the Olympics are going the way they're supposed to!*

Things had looked pretty scary when they started, but by the end, the U.S. team had finished fourth and qualified for the team finals.

Paul finished an impressive sixth in the individual all-around qualifier, so he and Blaine, who finished fourteenth, and Steve, at thirty-sixth, would advance to the individual all-around finals four days later. Paul told Morgan his goal was to finish in the top fifteen of the individual competition.

The men's team finals on September 18 were almost a repeat of the qualifiers. Blaine stepped out-of-bounds on floor, earning an automatic penalty. Then he missed a catch and fell off the high bar. This was a nightmare! Steve landed badly and reinjured an already-sore ankle. Sean managed to get the highest U.S. score, a 9.787 on parallel bars, but it wasn't enough to pull the team into medal contention.

Paul landed a good vault and parallel bars routine and finished thirteenth over-all. Morgan's best score was a decent 9.425 on the rings, but the brothers were both disappointed when the team finished in fifth place, the same as the U.S. squad had done in Atlanta. Gymnastic power-houses China, the Ukraine, and Russia were the medal winners in the team final.

Unfortunately, since medal expecta-tions had been so strong for the U.S. team, finishing out of the top three was a hard pill to swallow. Paul and Morgan knew they had nothing to be ashamed of, especially since this was their first inter-national meet, but it was hard not to feel down.

The guys tried to remain upbeat when they gave interviews—it was the Olympics, after all—but some of the veterans finally got a little testy after one too many ques-tions about being disappointed. As John explained it, "The fact we're still in fifth place is a tribute to how competitive the world of gymnastics is. . . . It's tough. . . . You can be a great team and be fifth. I think we're a great team and we're fifth."

Paul and Morgan just looked at going

home without a team medal as a challenge: it was up to them to make sure the *next* Olympic team could do it. They had four years to work with their team members and the up-and-coming gymnasts to develop the medal-winning skills that had somehow been missing in Sydney.

Because Paul had qualified for the individual all-arounds and Morgan hadn't, Paul felt like he was missing something when he walked into the arena—he was used to having Morgan there to help him stay focused through the events. At least he had his buddy Blaine to talk to and root for during each rotation.

Paul was in the unfortunate position of following Olympic champion Alexei Nemov on almost every event, and he said found the pressure a little nerve-racking. Nemov boasted six Olympic medals from the Atlanta games, and Paul tried hard not to watch him like a spectator but instead to analyze his performance like a competitor. Still, he couldn't get over how elegant Nemov was from beginning to end. "Everything from start to finish is professional," Paul commented, shaking his head as he described the experienced Russian's graceful performance. It was no surprise when Nemov won the individual all-around gold medal.

Paul managed to do one better than what he'd told Morgan he was aiming for, coming in fourteenth. If nothing else, Paul was going home to U.S. competitions with a ton more confidence. He knew that if he had survived these nerves, not much at home could throw him off. Besides, there were still the event finals, which were taking place on September 24, Paul and Morgan's birthday!

Morgan couldn't think of a better way to spend his birthday than competing in the floor exercise at the Olympics. It was definitely going to be hard to top that in the future!

Walking out onto the floor, Morgan had to catch his breath all over again. It was an amazing feeling to represent his country in front of all these people from so many nations.

Morgan stepped up, saluted the judges, and took a deep, calming breath before starting his first tumbling pass. Once he got moving, his body took over, executing the skills he had practiced for so long. He turned in a good routine, even though he landed a little short on his dismount, and he was happy with how he had performed. He finished in seventh place with a 9.262.

The Hamms' first Olympics was over, and although the team's results were a bit disappointing, the twins knew they had performed well.

The more-experienced guys on the team all tried hard to remind themselves that there was nothing wrong with doing your best on a given day and still not winning. But no matter what they said, it was tough for them to be the first men's team since 1972 to come home from the Olympics completely empty-handed. The truth was that it stung.

Medal or no medal, all of the guys took the Hamms out to celebrate their birthday. Although it wasn't their own private party, the twins admitted it was a pretty good one. It was hosted by *Sports Illustrated* magazine, and everyone was there! The festivities were on the waterfront, right next to the famous Sydney Opera House. They couldn't get over how spectacular that unique building was; all lit up at night, it looked like some kind of alien spaceship that had landed in the harbor. When the twins had first dreamed of going to the Olympics all those years ago, it hadn't occurred to them that it would mean such an exotic birthday celebration. They had a blast!

Before the competition was even

over, Morgan said he couldn't wait to get back into the gym and start working. Hey, wait, isn't that Paul's line? Apparently, seeing how well the international gymnasts could perform provided a whole new level of motivation for Morgan. He promised a ton of improvement over the next four years; he and Paul still had a lot more growing to do until they reached their peaks as gymnasts.

CHAPTER SEVEN

Facing Challenges

Morgan and Paul vowed they'd be back in four years with lots more experience, more strength, more-difficult routines, and, hopefully, some medal-winning performances.

U.S. Olympic coach Kormann, who announced his retirement from the Olympic program after the Sydney games, shared their optimism, saying, "I'm very confident some of the guys in this meet will be Olympic medalists. It's just that they're going to have to wait at least four years."

On the long plane trip home, the boys wondered how their lives would be different as a result of going to the Olympics. They didn't have to wait long to find out. While they had been pretty much just two regular guys at Waukesha South before they left for Australia, now everyone knew who they were. It turned out that the school had set up a giant-screen television so the students could all watch Morgan and Paul's Olympic performances.

They found that being at home was a little more exciting now, too. When they were out and about in Waukesha and even in Minneapolis, people recognized them. All of a sudden they had fans writing and e-mailing them, wanting to know all kinds of crazy things. People were asking about their favorite ice cream flavor (Morgan likes butter pecan or vanilla), what kind of cheese they eat (cheddar, you cheesehead! They're from Wisconsin), and who hogs the bathroom more (separate bathrooms).

Although the twins tried to answer all

their letters at first, sending out auto-
graphed photos with every response,
soon it fell to Sandy to take care of these
things because the boys were about to go
away . . . again! This time they were
going to be part of the T.J. Maxx Tour of
World Gymnastics Champions.

Hey, wasn't that where they first got a
taste of the big time, way back in 1996?
Uh-huh! It was only four years ago, but it
seemed like a different lifetime. This time
they were the big men on campus, fresh
from making their Olympic debut.

The tour, which began on October 12
in Reno, Nevada, would go to thirty-one
cities over fifty-one days, ending in
Anaheim in December. It included gold
and silver medalists from the Russian
team as well as a number of American
gymnasts, like Blaine and John. The for-
mat was non-competitive; in fact, it was
all fun, including *multiple* gymnasts on
the parallel bars and high bar at the same

time! You'll never see that in Olympic competition!

The show, which took a full week of twelve-hour days to rehearse and get ready, included lights, music, costumes, and lots of fancy choreography. It was designed as a chance for all the gymnasts to have a great time and show off their favorite moves and to bring live gymnastics to new audiences.

Not only were Morgan and Paul looking forward to having fun on the tour, it also paid well. They figured they'd earn about half the cost of their upcoming college educations in the eight-week tour. Of course, since the twins were earning money for their sport, they had to accept that they wouldn't be able to compete in the NCAA at college. College athletes must have amateur status in order to compete, and as soon as an athlete is paid for something involving his sport, he becomes professional.

So when Paul and Morgan decided to do the tour, it meant that they were turning professional and planning to earn their living from doing gymnastics. But it certainly seemed a safe bet they'd made the right choice!

The tour's high point for the twins was a performance in Milwaukee. They were thrilled by the deafening roar when they took the floor for the first time as Olympians in the Bradley Center.

Paul and Morgan couldn't believe they had turned into such celebrities right there in their hometown. Not only that, but while the tour was in Milwaukee, they were honored with a parade and a rally hosted by Waukesha South High School. They even got a key to the city. After all, not every city can say it's home to an Olympian, let alone two!

The T.J. Maxx tour ended in mid-December with a performance in front of a huge and enthusiastic crowd in

Anaheim. The boys had really enjoyed themselves, but they were ready to stop riding the tour bus and living in hotels for a while.

After all, they had an awful lot of planning to do, figuring out how they were going to finish high school and what they were going to do about college. Plus they were looking forward to going back to work with Coach Maloney. The next Olympics were just four years off!

Four years might seem like a long time to be planning ahead, but fighting to be the best gymnast in the world is a pretty intense task. Luckily Paul and Morgan both realized that the T.J. Maxx tour had actually helped them in some ways. Performing five times a week in a different city practically every day was a great way to gain confidence. Paul had always described himself as a bit shy, but by the time they were done with the tour, both brothers were much more outgoing.

Paul balances on the rings with razor-sharp precision.

Paul is always happy to sign autographs for eager fans.

Paul on the parallel bars at the 2000 Men's Gymnastics Trials, where Paul and Morgan both helped their squad make it to the Olympic competition.

Paul becomes the first American men's gymnast to capture a World Championships gold medal. (Standing on the podium with silver medalist Yang Wei of China [left] and Hiroyuki Tomita of Japan [right], who took home the bronze.)

Paul and Morgan really are two of a kind!

Can you tell them apart? Some say Paul (right) has more freckles.

Paul's strongest events are the high bar and the pommel horse. Morgan excels at the floor routine.

Morgan defies gravity on the rings.

Morgan's moves drive the crowd wild.

Morgan stays strong under pressure.

Morgan stays balanced as he reaches for Athens.

One of the things the twins had noticed in Sydney was how hard it was *not* to watch the guys who ended up winning medals. They had . . . charisma. That's why it was so important for the Hamms to keep getting out in front of audiences and performing. They could learn just by the crowd reactions what it was that grabbed an audience's attention. And no matter what judges said about how they worked, they were an audience, too, and they responded to a good performance. Coach Maloney knew it, USA Gymnastics knew it, and the twins were learning all about it.

When it came time to go to the first post-Olympic team training camp in December in Colorado Springs, no one needed to tell the twins they had matured. Morgan and Paul couldn't get over how much higher their confidence level was than the year before. And that was important, because this camp was where they would start learning the new skills that they would need to include in their routines for the next four years.

Wait, didn't they know enough skills already? Well, maybe, but no matter how many they knew, they had to keep learning, because the skills gymnasts use in competition keep changing.

Any move that any gymnast includes in a routine has to be one that's approved by the FIG—part of the FIG *Code of Points*. And just in case people start to think the Olympics or the World Championships are too easy, every four years the FIG gets together and finds ways to make gymnastics more difficult. It's called changing the code. It doesn't seem very fair, but it's the way it works.

So every four years, each national gymnastics federation has to teach its athletes and coaches these new moves. That's one of the things that was happening at that team training camp in December 2000.

Now they were back to their regular

routine of twice-a-day workouts with Coach Maloney at Swiss Turners and were trying to finish high school while they kept improving at their sport.

Getting through their daily schedule was just one way the boys showed their dedication to gymnastics. Each school day, they would drive to South High School, take two classes in the morning, then drive thirty minutes to the gym to work out for two hours. Then they would eat lunch, drive thirty minutes back to school, and take two more classes. At the end of the school day, it was back in the car to drive the same thirty minutes *back* to the gym for their afternoon training. Like most teenagers, the twins argued about who was going to drive—but in their case, neither of them wanted to be the one! Each one would rush to get to the car first so he could grab the "shotgun" passenger seat and get some extra rest while the other had to drive.

When they were done with their afternoon workouts, they headed home and finished their homework. At that point they fell into bed to get rested and ready to start all over again. A schedule like that didn't leave too much time for goofing around, but the Hamms weren't really concerned with goofing around. They were totally focused on becoming the best gymnasts in the world.

The twins planned to go to college near home so they could keep training at Swiss Turners with Coach Maloney. They were considering Marquette University or the University of Wisconsin (both in Milwaukee), but even their parents agreed that college would probably be put on hold if they made the World Championship team.

Morgan and Paul had skipped the Winter Cup, having established their places on the U.S. Senior team with their Olympic performances. So their first step in getting to the World Championships was the Pontiac American Team Cup in Honolulu, Hawaii, at the end of March.

Hawaii, huh? This job of being a professional gymnast wasn't too bad after all.

The meet would bring together athletes from the United States, China, and Romania and was a good opportunity to start to work routines that included the new difficulties specified in the FIG *Code of Points*. And, everyone agreed, the new code was *much* more difficult.

The guys all had a chance to enjoy Hawaii before they got down to business: they visited the USS *Missouri* memorial at Pearl Harbor and even tried surfing! Although they loved the beach and the ocean, the twins decided they'd be better off sticking to gymnastics.

As they took the competition floor, Morgan and Paul couldn't help but compare the difference in the atmosphere from the T.J. Maxx tour. Gone were the loud music, flashing lights, and group routines. Though there was a performance of native Hawaiian dancers before the meet started and very enthusiastic fans, this couldn't be confused with an exhibition: this was a competition.

Yes, the tour had been a lot of fun, but it felt good to be back to serious gymnastics.

Morgan found that he was a little rough in his first event, pommel horse. In fact, the whole U.S. team started slowly, and Romania led after the first rotation. Then the guys hit their stride and started turning in the routines they were capable of. The United States pulled ahead in rotation two and never looked back. Winning five of six events, the U.S. team beat China, with Romania in third. Olympic teammate Sean Townsend earned the highest all-around score, ahead of Paul in second and Morgan in third.

Although Paul had finished ahead of

Morgan, Morgan had tied with another U.S. athlete for the top floor exercise score. In all, USA Gymnastics was happy with the team's performance.

Unfortunately, that was the high point of the twins' 2001 season.

One day in early June, Morgan was struggling to master a parallel bars move called a double back. He swung his body up and over the bars, then switched his grip, as he'd been practicing. But this time, his timing was off. Suddenly his whole body was on track for disaster, and before he knew it, he'd crashed, catching the bar hard with his shoulder.

Morgan felt a sharp shooting pain under his arm and in his back, and then his whole shoulder went numb. He dropped from the bars onto the padded mats, clutching his arm to his side in agony.

Morgan was used to pain: some of the moves he and his brother did on the parallel bars hurt even when they did them *right*. But this was different. He couldn't feel his shoulder.

He'd never been hurt like this before.

Injuries, including major ones, are common in gymnastics, and Paul and Morgan both knew it. But until that moment, the twins had been lucky, with no serious injuries slowing them down. Given how hard they were pushing themselves to learn new skills and improve their techniques, though, once the injury finally happened, it seemed it had been almost inevitable.

After much consulting over Morgan's strange symptom of numbness, the doctors concluded that he had stretched a nerve that was affecting his ability to use one of his shoulder muscles. Sadly, the only thing he could do was rest it to see if it got better. He was allowed to do some strength and conditioning work but no gymnastics.

No gymnastics?? Then what else was there?

Morgan's first resolution was that no gymnastics wouldn't mean he'd stop going to the gym. He was there every day, stretching and working his legs and body, trying to maintain as much of his fitness, flexibility, and strength as he could. He did physical therapy for his shoulder every day, and he spent time with Paul, helping with Paul's workouts, talking about skills and routines. Morgan was doing his best to be a gymnast . . . without doing gymnastics.

But he was worried that he wasn't going to make it back into shape in time for the U.S. Championships. Here it was mid-June, and that meet was in August in Philadelphia. He *had* to compete there if he was going to make it to the World Championships!

While Morgan was figuring out how to work around his shoulder injury, Paul was continuing to work toward the U.S. Championships. Several weeks after Morgan's injury, Paul was at a training camp, working out with the other members of the men's team.

One day, while doing a round-off (a simple move—a lot like a cartwheel— that gymnasts use as a lead-in to those difficult back handsprings and flips), Paul felt a sharp pain in the lower part of his right leg. He'd been experiencing some nagging soreness in his right ankle for some time, but this was much worse. Fear washed over him at the idea that he'd ignored a small problem and was being punished by a far worse one.

He immediately had the team trainers and coach look at his leg and was relieved when they guessed it was some kind of sprain. But deep down, Paul sensed that wasn't the case. His worries seemed valid when the leg didn't improve after being wrapped and iced regularly.

Finally it was time to go to the doctor. Paul held his breath while he waited for the verdict, and when he heard the news, his heart sank.

Paul had a fracture in his tibia—a broken leg. Even though the pain had been severe, Paul still couldn't believe it. He had been doing gymnastics right up until that moment. He couldn't have a broken leg. He didn't have *time* for a broken leg! "All I did was a round-off, Coach!" he protested, unable to comprehend that such a basic move had caused something so serious.

But the truth couldn't be denied—both Paul and Morgan now had injuries that could hold them back from the incredible heights they'd seemed right on the verge of reaching.

CHAPTER EIGHT
Coming Back

It was tough not to be discouraged by their injuries, but Paul and Morgan were determined not to let the challenge stop them.

For Morgan, that still mostly meant just resting his shoulder. But one way to help Paul's fracture heal faster was to have a pin surgically inserted. He wasn't happy about it, but he agreed that it seemed like the right thing to do. The good news was that instead of a cast, the doctors gave him a supportive boot, so he could get around okay. Each day, in addition to Paul's upper-body workout and stretching, trainers removed his boot and attached electrical stimulation electrodes to his leg to speed his recovery.

With both of the twins rehabbing injuries, they really had to help each other to keep their morale up. It seemed like they were spending as much time in physical therapy as they were doing gymnastics. They agreed that if that was what they had to do to get healthy, then that was what they would do. And they'd try not to complain about it too much.

Every gymnast they knew had gone through some kind of injury and rehab. John Roethlisberger had a rebuilt knee; Jason Gatson's knee was almost bionic after several surgeries! Blaine had shoulder problems (in fact, he was out again with another torn shoulder and was going to miss the 2001 U.S. Championships and Worlds), and there were any number of young guys who got hurt and just never came back. So the Hamms weren't going to whine about it; they were just going to do what it took to get back to competing.

The Hamms' injuries were clearly going to keep them from being ready for the all-arounds at the U.S. Championships, but they had to get to at least one event to qualify for the Worlds. Coach Maloney decided to make lemonade with these lemons—he and Paul would use the time to improve on Paul's worst event, rings, since that was one that wasn't affected by the leg injury. That way, Paul would get his event in at the U.S. Championships and improve his skills while he was getting there.

Coach Maloney had hoped that Morgan could compete on pommel horse, which would put the least amount of strain on his shoulder. But even after all the resting and stretching, Morgan's shoulder was still frustratingly numb. At one point, as hard as he tried, he couldn't even lift his arm above his head! The problem was that nerves heal more slowly than just about anything else in the body, and the only thing he could do was wait for them to repair themselves.

Morgan got so tired of waiting for his shoulder to recover, there were times he actually considered quitting gymnastics. "My shoulder just kept getting smaller and smaller and I thought gymnastics might be over for me," he later confessed. But Paul wouldn't hear of it; he just kept reminding Morgan of the thrill of the Olympics and how he had proved himself to be world class. Besides, Paul told him, he might be able to find another workout partner, but there would never be anyone who would help him as much as Morgan.

It was hard for Paul to head to Philadelphia for the U.S. Championships knowing that Morgan couldn't even feel his shoulder. It meant Morgan was going to miss the 2001 World Championships, too, so Paul decided he was going to have to compete well enough for both of them.

Paul made it through the Philadelphia meet, doing his rings routine and getting the score he needed to be considered for one of the committee-selected spots for the Worlds team.

The first four competitors got automatic berths on the team. That meant that Olympic teammate and brand-new national champion Sean Townsend, along with Brett McClure, Steve McCain, and NCAA champ Raj Bhavsar, would be going. The committee also picked Guard Young, who had finished fifth, and named Paul Hamm as the sixth member of the team.

Paul was relieved that the committee was giving him a spot. Even though he was recovering from an injury, Paul just knew that he'd be ready for the meet, which was in Ghent, Belgium, in November. He had two whole months to prepare.

Though his ankle troubled him, Paul felt better and better in training before the team left for Ghent. He was definitely psyched to go to Worlds, where they were going to try to win a team medal for the first time since 1979. Sure, it would seem weird going to such a big international meet without Blaine, John, and especially Morgan, but he was still ready to do his best.

The World Championships was a huge meet, with more than 300 athletes on forty national teams in qualifying rounds. The U.S. team needed to finish in the top eight to move to the finals, and the first thirty-eight individual scores would advance to the all-around. As the team worked out and got to spend time together, Paul was excited, because it was clear that there was a lot of talent among them and the chemistry was great—the guys were really having a good time, and their gymnastics looked, well, world class!

Paul knew that he and the rest of the

guys had worked as hard as they could to be totally prepared. He was sure this team could get the job done and come home with a medal. And they set right out to do it.

They couldn't get over how enthusiastic the spectators were. Having an audience cheer when they nailed their routines was a huge boost. The guys started out strong, leading each event with high scores. Steve wowed the judges with his vault, earning the high score for that event, and Sean even hit his parallel bars routine for a 9.787.

They led Belarus by a tiny margin all the way through the fifth rotation, when Paul's high bar gremlins paid him a visit—he missed a catch and fell, and he had to remount to finish his routine. Perfection remained elusive when Raj and Guard had problems in their floor exercises, but all the guys knew they had performed really well, had pretty much gone out and hit what they had to hit . . . and they finished in second place in the qualifying round!

Despite the small errors, it felt like things had gone just their way. They had started the meet knowing that the field was wide open, and here they were in second place. "It's great!" said Paul. "But," he pointed out, "it's all about hitting it in the finals." They were up against the best in the world: Belarus, Korea, Romania, the Ukraine, France, China, and Russia.

In addition to team success, Paul and his 2000 Olympic teammates Sean and Steve advanced to the individual all-around. Paul had been through some really tough times to get to this meet, but now the effort seemed worthwhile.

The team had a day off to rest, stretch, and get ready for the team finals. And ready they were!

The U.S. men started out on pommel

horse and had some tense moments as Paul had a hard time with his routine, only scoring an 8.412. Shaking it off, he came right back with a strong rings routine and got things back in sync. The team kept up their concentration, with good vaults and parallel bars, and Paul made up for his preliminary round high bar mistake by nailing all of his release moves for a 9.373.

The pressure of being in medal contention and the adrenaline they all felt trying to hit their routines seemed to be working for them.

They just had floor exercise left, and they must have been trying so hard to hit everything as big as they could, they ended up making some errors. Sean lost his balance and sat down on his first tumbling routine, and Paul stepped out-of-bounds twice.

When all the scores were in, the U.S. team had won high bar and was second on rings, third on parallel bars, and fourth in the floor and vault. And what did that add up to? The U.S. team's first-ever silver medal in a World Championships!

They had finished less than three points behind Belarus and 1.3 points ahead of Ukraine. As Paul described it later, "We just kept going and kept fighting and never gave up."

Paul expressed everyone's feelings when he said, "It's been a hard year, but we got it done." He was especially thinking of the guys who weren't there: his brother and his friends Blaine and John.

But although the team had its hardware, the work wasn't done. Paul, Sean, and Steve still had individual all-arounds to look forward to.

The individual finals started out well. They were hitting their routines and feeling loose and strong. By the time they got to the final rotation, high bar, Sean was in first and Paul was in third. Right in there fighting with them for medals were China's Feng Jing and the two-time champion Russian Ivan Ivankov.

Paul could see that Sean was feeling the pressure as he chalked his hands and strapped on his grips. Still, Paul felt really good about his chances. Right up until he saw his friend and teammate miss a release move and slip off the high bar . . . and right out of medal contention. Paul couldn't find words to say to console Sean, and he knew he had to shake off what he had just seen because he was up next.

Trying to clear the image of Sean's fall from his mind, Paul prepared himself, saluted, and started his routine. He felt pretty good, releasing and catching, swinging and rotating. But in one split second, his timing went off and all of a sudden, the bar wasn't in his hands when it should have been. He felt his face smash into the bar and then he crashed to the mat. Lying there, feeling the blood oozing from his nose, Paul couldn't believe it was over. The United States wasn't going to win an all-around World Championship medal after all.

When the scores were tallied, Paul and Sean had literally fallen to seventh and eighth, a huge disappointment after starting out the round so strong. But Coach Maloney kept reminding Paul of how far he had come back from a broken leg just months ago. "The fact that you were in there to win shows what kind of gymnast you are," Coach told him.

The whole team was there to cheer their teammates on in the event finals: Steve in floor exercise and Sean in parallel bars. Steve put on a great show but finished just out of the medals in fourth place. Sean, however, put the emotions of the individual all-arounds behind him and turned in a beautiful routine for a score of 9.70. He had won the first U.S. men's individual event gold medal at the World Championships since 1979!

As Paul stood watching his friend on the top of the medal stand while the U.S. national anthem played, he could feel his disappointment over yesterday's mistake turning into pure motivation. He was thrilled for Sean . . . and he wanted to be the next one to win a World Championship medal!

Well, thought Paul, *time to go back to the gym and get ready for next year.*

CHAPTER NINE

Recharged Hopes

Paul came home from the World Championships with mixed feelings. It was an amazing feeling to be part of the silver medal team, but he was having a hard time shaking his disappointment over his fall from the high bar. At least he was happy to get back to the gym with Morgan and Coach Maloney and to re-dedicate himself to improving his skills and developing new routines.

Meanwhile, 2002 brought a big change for Paul and Morgan outside of gymnastics: they had finally finished high school, and they moved into an apartment in Milwaukee, right near the University of

Wisconsin, which they had started to attend.

This was the boys' first apartment on their own, and it took some getting used to. All of a sudden it was up to them, not Mom or Dad, to make sure the bills were paid on time, keep the kitchen stocked with groceries, and clean up the house. For the most part, they were enjoying it, and they were only a half hour away from home, so they could visit when they wanted and get a familiar mom-cooked meal.

Paul's first semester of college started in January, and he was taking a light course load of thirteen credits so he could spend lots of time training. Morgan, who still went to the gym every day despite his bad shoulder—he claimed it was the only thing that kept him sane—had started attending classes in the fall semester when it was clear that he was not going to be able to compete. Paul teased him that he was looking for a cure for his shoulder by taking anatomy and physiology classes. What was wrong with that? Morgan wondered.

While Morgan was trying to find ways to stay occupied, Paul was working with him and Coach Maloney to upgrade his routines. Keeping the 2003 World Championships and the 2004 Olympics in sight, he knew it was important to work on skills that were going to help him win and to keep Morgan's head in the game.

Paul was doing new routines on floor, pommel horse, and parallel bars. Coach Maloney said that Paul's new floor exercise was one of the hardest ones in the world (it even included some break-dancing moves that were sure to please the crowd!). If he could hit it, his scores would be hard to beat.

It was important for Paul to get comfortable with all these new routines at the beginning of the season because, as good as he was, doing new moves made him nervous until he had done them a bunch of times in competition.

The plan was that he would try them out at a small meet at the beginning of February and then take them to Las Vegas for the Winter Cup in mid-February. That would help him feel ready for the Visa American Cup at the beginning of March, a prestigious invitational meet (with good prize money!) that includes four American men and four American women competing against athletes from several different countries.

Knowing that tough work was ahead, Paul went to the Winter Cup, hoping for a win. Todd Thornton, the 2000 junior champion who was new to the Senior all-around team at the Winter Cup, had other ideas. Todd fought Paul through every rotation, finally pulling ahead of Paul in the sixth, where Todd nailed his floor exercise and got a 9.8, the highest mark of the meet. That was too tough for Paul to beat;

he had to be satisfied with second place.

There was some consolation in the fact that Paul succeeded in beating Todd in the floor event final. He nailed his two difficult layout double-doubles—twisting double flips with his body completely straight— earning a 9.7 and first place. He also won the vault event gold medal. Despite the all-around silver medal, Paul was pleased with how his new routines had gone.

It was obvious watching all the competitors that everyone was working to upgrade their routines. There were lots of new skills, and the athletes were improving the way they executed them. Everyone in Senior men's gymnastics was looking toward Athens in 2004, where the United States was going to do its best to erase the disappointment of Sydney and come home with a medal.

In March, Paul headed to Orlando for the Visa American Cup. As ready as he felt, he knew there'd be stiff competition from the representatives from Bulgaria, the Ukraine, Cuba, France, and Japan—especially Russian Alexei Nemov, whom Paul had found to be so impressive at the Sydney Olympics.

Of course, there was good reason for Paul to have been impressed: Nemov had been to two Olympics and had won a total of twelve—yep, count 'em, twelve—Olympic medals, including a gold medal in individual all-around and high bar in Sydney and a team all-around gold from Atlanta, as well as a gold in the vault in those 1996 games. The only thing Nemov was missing was a world championship, and he hadn't given up on it yet. Jeez! Where did he keep all of that hardware!?

Paul still appreciated Nemov's power and skill, but he was no longer awestruck when he competed against him. He was just focused on beating the Russian.

Focus was clearly a good thing, because after executing his new routines well and scoring consistently high, Paul was able to beat Alexei Nemov in Orlando!

Unfortunately, he still didn't manage to grab the gold in any individual event, and Cuba's Eric Lopez beat him by 0.375 to win his second Visa American Cup title. Still, a silver medal was something Paul could be proud of, especially since he'd at least overcome the intimidation of Nemov.

Paul headed back to the gym to continue getting ready for his next international meet, the Pacific Alliance Championships in May.

That was one more meet Morgan would have to miss. Morgan couldn't believe it had been over a year since he'd last competed, back in March 2001! The good news was that Coach Maloney and the doctors had finally said that Morgan was on his way to competing again. He was just going to have to build up slowly, but at least all the waiting was over—he could start real workouts again.

Paul was thrilled for his brother and couldn't wait to compete alongside him again. In the meantime, he made an important step in his own career at the Pacific Alliance Championships, grabbing some huge wins to boost his confidence back up.

First, the U.S. team won the all-around team competition. Paul notched his highest-ever score in the still rings (9.600), showing that the extra work there had really paid off. He grabbed gold in the all-around, took first on vault, and tied for first on high bar. He even came in third on floor exercise!

Paul realized that he was beginning to beat the gymnasts he had watched in awe when he and Morgan had been in Sydney: first Nemov at the Visa American Cup, and now at the Pacific Alliance meet he'd finished ahead of Yang Wei of China, the silver medalist in the 2000 Olympics.

There was no doubt about it—Paul Hamm was back, and better than ever!

It felt amazing to be told that he looked light-years ahead of where he had been two years ago at the Olympics. Still, he needed to keep winning big meets if he was going to accomplish his goal, which was to win an all-around medal at the 2003 World Championships and then at the 2004 Olympic Games. Paul finally believed those titles were within his grasp.

With his win in Vancouver, Paul could turn his focus on the U.S. Championships, which would take place in Cleveland, Ohio, in August. And the best part of all was that Paul wasn't going alone—Morgan was back in action at last!

Even though he hadn't been competing, Morgan had been maturing. And whether he went to meets or not, he was in the gym every day with one of the best coaches and one of the best gymnasts in the country. He had a pretty clear idea of where he stood, and he felt good about it. Morgan had spent so much time working on the strengths that he could practice and improving his overall endurance, he had a new confidence in his ability to perform well.

When they got back on the mats together at a warm-up in Cleveland, Paul and Morgan felt like something had finally been set right—they were back in competition together. Morgan was happy and relieved to be competing again, glad he had let Paul talk him out of quitting. He knew his brother was strong and ready to win the U.S. Championships, so they were looking forward to a great meet.

Paul knew the win was anything but guaranteed. Blaine Wilson had nabbed the title five times already and had only missed it the previous year because he hadn't been able to compete after an injury. No one else had ever won the event when Blaine was competing. This year Blaine was healthy, and he wanted his title back, especially because it would be a record sixth.

Still, Paul was confident he was ready to beat his friend. He had high start values and he had been nailing his skills in his workouts. And his brother was back with him, which made him very happy. *Bring it on*, he thought. *I'm ready!*

Despite the fact that Blaine had a hyperextended knee, he started off strong and built up a good lead after two events. But then Blaine started to make mistakes and Paul was right there behind him, hitting his routines as practiced. Paul was frustrated when he had a slip off the high bar, but Blaine had two falls on floor and Paul finished the prelims ahead of Blaine, in first place, that much closer to winning the national championship title.

Morgan, who was competing in all events (even though he had to hold out a little to avoid problems with his shoulder), had a good day, too, ending up in fifth place at the end of the preliminaries. Not bad for his first big meet in a year! Of course it didn't hurt that he turned in an awesome floor routine for a 9.950. That floor routine didn't look like Morgan had missed a day of training, let alone a whole year!

For the finals, Paul and Morgan were in the same rotation as Blaine, so everyone could watch closely as Paul and Blaine duked it out head-to-head. The crowd cheered like crazy for both gymnasts. They went wild after Blaine's stunning high bar routine, which earned him a 9.90 and a congratulatory high five from Paul.

High bar was where Paul had had a problem in the preliminary round, and he was determined that there would be no mistakes in the finals. So he made a quick decision to leave out one of his releases, just to be safe. It lowered the start value of the exercise but kept him from risking a major problem. The end result was a solid 9.65, but the crowd made it clear they thought he deserved better!

Paul was pretty excited by the time they got to the floor exercise. He even pumped his fist in celebration as he left the mat, realizing that his overall results seemed to be stronger than Blaine's.

Paul watched the scoreboard for the final results, but he knew in his heart he had reached yet another of his goals. When the scores were posted, Paul's dream had come true: he was U.S. national champion.

Yes!

It had been an incredible meet, a battle between friends that was fun to fight, especially for Paul in the end! In addition to the all-around lead, Paul had placed first on pommel horse (9.7) and on vault (9.6). All thoughts of his ankle injury from last year were gone. He was on top of the world—well, at least the USA!

Even though Paul had been convinced

he could beat Blaine, he was still over-whelmed as he thought about what it meant. He remembered being fourteen years old and watching Blaine win his first U.S. Championships on television. And here Paul was now, winning *his* first title. The first, he hoped, of many.

While Morgan's victories weren't as splashy as Paul's, the U.S. Champion-ships proved to be more than just a "try it and see what happens" meet for him as well. He had wanted to finish in the top six but actually came in fourth in the all-around. Plus he snagged an amazing 9.95 in the floor exercise in *both* the prelims and the finals, not only beating Paul in that event, but winning the national title for floor, too.

Coach Stacy Maloney couldn't have been prouder of his two star students. He knew they were right on track for the next big challenge.

CHAPTER TEN

Hometown,
Home Country

It was time for some fun after all the pressure of the U.S. Championships—the Hamm twins were headed out to Anaheim, California, for a low-key international meet, the T.J. Maxx USA vs. the World show. The meet, a fund-raiser for the Special Olympics, was held at the Arrowhead Pond stadium, which would be the site of the 2003 World Championships. Of course, the exhibition wasn't *all* about fun, since it was also an opportunity for gymnasts to perform in the Worlds arena, warming up for the contest to come.

The enthusiastic audience and light tone of the event promised a good, relaxing time for Paul and Morgan, which they both really needed at that point!

Morgan was having a great time on his specialty, the floor exercise, thrilling the crowd with a layout double-double, part of one of his awesome tumbling passes. Then suddenly his feet hit the mat wrong, and he felt like he had landed on cement. He collapsed as pain shot right up both of his legs.

Oh, no! Not again!!

Paul watched in horror as Morgan was taken from the arena for x-rays. He waited, as anxious as he knew his brother had to be, to hear the results. Finally the news came that it was just a pair of sprains. Morgan had recovered quickly from sprains in the past, so the brothers hoped that would hold true this time. Still, it was an injury all the same, and Morgan was once again out of commission for a time.

While Morgan focused on rehab and limited workouts, Paul took a trip to the French Open Tournament in Paris, where he succeeded in beating a lot of big international names for a win on high bar. He also finished fifth in floor exercise.

When November rolled around, Morgan wasn't quite ready for the 2002 World Championships, taking place in Debrecen, Hungary. Paul would have to attend the event alone. But this year wasn't nearly as major as the 2001 competition had been. World champion team events and all-around awards are only contested in odd years, so the 2002 Worlds was for individual event medals only. Paul set out to compete without Morgan at his side and finished third in floor exercise.

As 2002 came to a close, both brothers had their eyes on the two years ahead—they knew that 2003 and 2004 could be *their* years if everything went as well as they hoped.

Right from the beginning of 2003 it was clear that the twins' focus was on two events—the U.S. Championships, which were coming to Milwaukee in June, and then the World Championships, which would be held in Anaheim in August.

The Hamms were psyched because they'd have the hometown advantage for the U.S. Championships and then the home *country* advantage for the World Championships. Some people think there's some "home" advantage in the judging, but no matter what, there's definitely a bonus to having a crowd rooting you on!

Morgan's shoulder was still a factor, as it would never heal completely. But his bad landing at the T.J. Maxx meet in Anaheim was proving to be more of a problem than he had anticipated. He had to limit his workouts for almost six months so he didn't add any stress to his ankles, which were still bothering him when he tumbled. At least floor exercise was his strong event, so he didn't feel like he'd be too far behind when he was able to go all out again. But it was so frustrating to be waiting to heal . . . again!

Just as they had the last time Morgan had coped with an injury, he and Coach Maloney concentrated on improving Morgan's other skills. In the last year they had certainly gotten a lot of practice learning to be patient—and creative—when dealing with injuries.

Unfortunately, that kind of experience was about to become really important.

In February, Paul was practicing a move called a cross on rings. Once again, it wasn't a terribly difficult move, but somehow his timing was a little off, and all at once he felt a sharp shooting pain in his left shoulder. He dropped to the mat, holding his arm, hoping to make the pain just disappear. This couldn't be happening to him! Not now! But when Coach

Maloney came to look at the injury, they both knew he had separated his shoulder.

The doctors did what they could, but Paul's shoulder joint had momentarily given out, resulting in a serious sprain. They said it would take about sixteen weeks for his shoulder to be fully recovered, and Paul calculated that sixteen weeks would bring him right up against the U.S. Championships. Not ideal, he and Coach Maloney agreed, but it could have been worse.

This time, it was Morgan who served as the role model for Paul. Paul told Morgan that he was using his brother's dedication during the long shoulder recovery as a model. If Morgan had kept at it and made it back to where he was, Paul certainly could.

In mid-April, Paul had a cortisone shot in his shoulder to try to reduce the swelling. It seemed to help, and he was able to start to use it a bit in his workouts, but this wasn't doing anything for his confidence.

Confidence was pretty important for the U.S. Championships, Paul knew. It certainly helped in dealing with the pressure of defending a national title!

Paul had a serious challenge ahead of him. Blaine was eager for another go at the title, and plenty of other guys were looking to prove themselves. Plus the event was a qualifier for the World Championships team—the top two finishers would guarantee their spots on the squad. The rest of the team would be chosen by a committee selection. Everyone wanted that guarantee, but no one more than Paul!

Paul, Morgan, and Coach Maloney talked about it and agreed that to be on the safe side, Paul would take a couple of skills out of his rings routine for the U.S. Championships. It would lower the start value but also lower the risk of reinjuring his shoulder.

With this in mind, the Hamms headed to a team training camp in the spring, where Paul and Morgan got a good look at Blaine and the rest of the guys they would face in Milwaukee in June. As always, the camp involved hard work, but it was good to see the rest of the team, work out with them . . . and check out where they were in their training. Paul was impressed by how good Blaine looked. He had close to 10.0 starts on every event, and he wasn't kidding about wanting his U.S. Championship title back. *Well*, thought Paul, *he's going to have to fight for it!*

Luckily, Paul did have that hometown advantage working for him. He and Morgan didn't have to travel: they would be able to stay at their own apartment since it was so close by. Also, they were already familiar with the U.S. Cellular Arena, where they'd be competing.

Their father had guaranteed that they'd have a lot of support, but it was like nothing Paul and Morgan had ever experienced—Sandy bought close to a hundred tickets for the boys' family, friends, and coworkers! Most of these people didn't usually get to see the twins compete in person, and they were prepared to cheer their lungs out.

The screams began the second Paul and Morgan walked out onto the floor. The brothers smiled and waved, giving their personal cheering section a special "hi" before getting down to business.

Their first rotation was the parallel bars. Paul turned in a good, solid routine; his shoulder felt like it was going to be okay.

He looked over to see that Blaine had gotten a 7.90—*really* low!—on his first event, the pommel horse. Paul knew he had to have had some kind of fall. Putting thoughts about what had happened aside, he turned his focus back to his own routines. Blaine's error had given

Paul a little breathing room, though Jason Gatson and Raj Bhavsar were both having a good meet and were right there behind him. Paul got more and more psyched as he hit skill after skill. The only place his score was low was on the rings, and that was partly due to the low start value of the routine to reduce the stress on his shoulder.

When the preliminary round was over, Paul was in first place by more than three-tenths of a point. Whew!

The surprise was that it was Jason Gatson, not Blaine, who was in second place. Though Blaine had done really well on the rest of his events, he couldn't overcome the low pommel horse score.

Morgan's main goal was to do well on floor, pommel horse, and vault. Those were his strengths, and that was where he and Coach Maloney thought he could be valuable in the selection committee's eyes as a World Championship team member. He had a good, strong preliminary round, finishing the day in fifth place, just over three-tenths of a point behind Guard Young.

Paul dazzled in the individual event finals, winning the pommel horse event with a 9.750 and racking up a second gold medal on the high bar.

Morgan was always motivated by competition, and in this meet, he and Paul were both "on" when it came to the floor exercise. Morgan laid down a beautiful routine, nailing his difficult dismount to a roar of approval from the crowd. When his score was posted, he reinforced his consistent superiority in floor by beating his brother for a second year in a row (this year by one-tenth of a point) to win the event.

The enthusiastic local fans couldn't lose—they were filled with hometown pride whenever the Hamms' names appeared on the scoreboard, and the twins gave them plenty of opportunity to express their support.

On finals day, Paul knew he had to be consistent, if not brilliant. He started out a little shaky on the floor exercise but then came right back with a very strong pommel horse routine. Once he made it through rings with an 8.9, he snuck a quick glance at the scoreboard. It looked like he was probably going to be okay.

Paul let the crowd's energy help him get psyched. Fans kept trying to get his attention for an autograph, and more than one group of girls shouted in unison that they loved him. It was so loud in the arena, it was incredible!

Even though he wasn't as strong as he would have liked to have been on parallel bars and high bar, Paul knew he had a one-point lead, which gave him some lee-way. Blaine once again had trouble with the pommel horse on the last rotation, and it was clear he wasn't going to nab the top spot. Jason Gatson, however, hit the parallel bars big. Would Jason walk away with the win?

Nope—not a chance! That one-point margin was more than enough to give Paul his second U.S. Championship, with Jason taking silver and Blaine forced to settle for bronze. Paul had done it—he'd held on to his title as national champ!

The win was especially sweet because Paul had done it in front of his parents and a hugely enthusiastic Milwaukee crowd. He'd also proved he was no one-hit wonder to any doubters who claimed that winning one national championship title could be a "fluke."

Morgan, meanwhile, had performed consistently and well on finals day, moving up a place to finish in fourth right behind Blaine. Coach Maloney was so proud of both of his boys!

Although the Hamm brothers were quite happy with the results of the U.S.

Championships, their work wasn't done yet. They had just two months to make sure their routines were truly world class—to put back the skills they had held back on to make sure they stayed healthy through the recent meet. Even though Morgan's place on the World Championship team wasn't assured, it never occurred to him not to work with Paul and Coach Maloney as if he were going to Worlds.

Shortly after the U.S. Championships, the boys headed out to Columbus, Ohio, for the selections.

The workouts were hard, especially since the guys were tired and drained from their recent big meet. But in the end, the selection committee named the third- through sixth-place finishers from the U.S. Championships to the Worlds team. That meant Morgan would be headed to Anaheim in August with Paul!

CHAPTER ELEVEN

The Worlds and Beyond

The World Championship preliminaries went as smoothly as Paul and Morgan could have hoped—Team USA finished in first place, ahead of Japan in second and defending team champion China in third! Not only that, but the U.S. squad was actually the only team to finish the preliminary round among the top ten as a team in every event. They were sixth or better on *every* apparatus.

Ready for more good news? Paul and Morgan were, and they weren't disappointed when Paul finished second and

Jason finished fourth to qualify for the all-around finals.

The men headed to the team finals feeling a lot of pressure even though (or was that because?) they were in first. There was no room for error with Japan and China right behind them; every hundredth of a point was going to count.

They started on floor exercise, and Paul and Morgan both hit their routines. The crowd went wild when Morgan did his break-dance sequence! The United States had the best team score in floor exercise. On to pommel horse, one of the team's weaker events. Both Morgan and Paul had good routines but not strong enough. China moved ahead of the United States after the second rotation. Jason had a tremendously strong rings routine, even adding a skill, and Blaine was awesome! China still led. Aargh!

On the fourth rotation, vault, the crowd (and the team) got really excited when the scores were posted and the United States was in first place. Their hopes came crashing down when it turned out there had been a scoring error on Morgan's vault.

Morgan had announced that he would do a Kassamatsu one-and-a-half with a start value of 9.9, but as he took off, he realized he wasn't going to get the full twist in, so he just did a Kassamatsu one-half, which had a start value of 9.5, and landed it safely.

At first the judges didn't notice the error and scored it with the higher start value, giving it a 9.562. Then U.S. coaches realized there had to be a mistake—the score was higher than the start value. They notified the officials, and when the score was adjusted (to a 9.152), the U.S. team was in second place, a disappointing place for them to be after thinking they were in first.

Morgan knew adjusting his skill in

the vault had been the right thing to do—
at least he'd gotten a decent score rather
than completely missing the vault. But he
couldn't help feeling bummed that if he'd
pulled off the tougher vault, his team
would have been in the top spot for real.

Sadly, even with strong routines on
parallel bars and high bar, Team USA just
couldn't raise their score enough to pull
back ahead of China. After an intense
and exciting six rotations, China beat the
United States by 0.875.

Paul, Morgan, and their teammates
had wanted gold, but it was pretty hard to
be disappointed with a second team silver
medal in two years—only the fourth-ever
team World Championships medal for the
United States. For Morgan, who hadn't
been in Ghent, it was an awesome experience to stand with his teammates and
receive the silver medal. And Paul cher-
ished this championship silver even more
than his first, because his brother had

been there with him, where he belonged!

Now it was time for Paul and Jason to turn their attention to the individual all-around finals.

Paul was pretty beat after team finals, but he had a day to rest, which helped. He thought about the fact that he was having the meet he had dreamed of (and planned for), hitting almost every skill and sticking his landings. He was exactly where he needed to be, mentally and physically, going into the all-around finals. And lingering worries about his exhaustion disappeared when his adrenaline kicked in the moment the crowd began to cheer for him. The audience roared its support, letting him know that they believed in him as much as he believed in himself. Paul listened to the cheers and let the noise wash over him, giving him energy to keep doing his best.

After five tough rotations, trading tenths of a point with China's Yang Wei and Japan's Hiroyuki Tomita, incredibly, it all came down to the high bar—just like it had in Ghent, two years ago, when Paul had fallen so badly and hurt himself. Talk about déjà vu! Of course, it was crucial for Paul to rewrite history and finish the event differently this time.

Paul did his best to put the memory of 2001 out of his head, and Coach Maloney worked hard to keep him psyched. Paul, too lost in his own thoughts, didn't even watch China's Yang Wei perform a near-flawless high bar routine.

Finally Yang Wei landed, and it was time for Paul to conquer his high bar demons.

Coach Maloney, normally pretty quiet, was in Paul's face, getting him pumped up. "You can do this; just go out and do the routine of your life! You've practiced this; just do what you know you can do!" Coach was saying. "They've got the team gold; we're going to get the all-around!"

Paul nodded and listened, trying to quell his nerves and think about his routine. Stepping up to the podium, he chalked his hands, took a deep breath, and saluted.

Paul's routine had five release skills, with four of them in a sequence. During the week, Paul had left out a release on the high bar because he just hadn't felt right. He knew that now, if he wanted to beat Yang, he had to do all five and do them perfectly.

He began his routine. Incredibly, everything felt right. Paul gained confidence as he went along. He started his release series, and he knew he was in the zone.

Release, catch. Release, catch. Release, catch. Release, twist and . . . catch! *Yes!*

When he stuck his landing, the crowd went wild. Paul knew he had won before anything flashed on the scoreboard. He had needed a 9.712 to beat Yang, and he had earned a 9.775.

Paul was the first-ever World Champion from the United States!

Coach Maloney, who had worked himself into a frenzy getting Paul psyched, exploded off his chair and gave Paul a huge bear hug. Paul got a hug from Jason, too, who had finished in eighth place.

Paul searched the crowd to find the athletes' box and saw Morgan, who had been so nervous watching, he almost couldn't stand it. He, along with everyone else, was on his feet, cheering. Morgan screamed so loud, he lost his voice! There was no one else in the universe Morgan wanted to see win a World Championship more than his twin brother.

The victory was so thrilling for both Paul and Morgan, they almost forgot that the championship week wasn't over yet—there were still event finals to be contested. Paul was competing in floor exercise, Jason on rings, and Blaine on rings and parallel bars. Morgan, unfortunately, had taken a rare fall in the preliminary floor exercise, which meant he hadn't qualified for the event finals. But he was still on cloud nine from the team's silver medal and his brother's triumph, so he happily took his place in the stands, ready to cheer his brother on . . . with what little voice he had left!

Amazingly, even after everything Paul had already accomplished and how worn out he had to be, he still turned in an incredible floor exercise routine. He was loose and relaxed and hit skill after skill, almost as if he felt he had to fill in on the event his brother normally shone in! Paul's score of 9.762 tied Jordan Jovtchev of Bulgaria for the gold, giving him another medal to bring home. Blaine finished sixth in both of his events, with Jason right behind Blaine on the rings.

As if being two-time national and now *world* champion weren't enough, USA

Gymnastics soon added another honor to the list, naming Paul Athlete of the Year—2003 was the year of the Hamms!

Paul and Morgan couldn't have written a better plan for getting to their next Olympics—recover from injuries, win a U.S. championship or two, win a team silver medal at the World Championships, and top it off with an individual title.

What next? Well, there was still some work to do, but now both twins felt like it they were definitely on the right road . . . to Athens, together.

CHAPTER TWELVE
Time for a Change

Paul returned from Anaheim in a bit of a daze, trying to absorb the fact that he was actually the world champion. It was beyond awesome to have realized a dream that he'd held close for so long.

After Worlds, USA Gymnastics organized a Tour of Champions, similar to the T.J. Maxx tour. Of course they wanted their new world champion to participate, but having worked so hard to get to the U.S. Championships and Worlds, Paul really felt he had to stay home. First of all, he was tired. Second of all, he wanted to keep up his training. After all, the Olympics were only a year off.

It was hard for him to say no; it was something he wasn't used to. He always enjoyed those tours and believed it was important to help promote the sport of gymnastics, especially men's gymnastics, which receives such a small amount of attention in this country. But if nothing else, Paul wanted to finish up at least this semester of school. He joked that at the rate he was going, it was going to take him ten years to get an undergraduate degree.

Paul and Morgan worked out at the gym and did schoolwork. As world champion, Paul put in some appearances for sponsors of various USA Gymnastics programs and even went to Belgium for a European exhibition. He thought it was pretty cool that the fans *there* recognized him—he got a fair number of autograph requests at the show.

Then in November 2003, Paul and Morgan made a decision that stunned the gymnastics world—they decided to change coaches.

After working with Coach Maloney at Swiss Turners for almost thirteen years, Paul and Morgan, along with their parents, simply felt the need to try something different. They had experienced a lot of success and pretty much learned everything they knew from Coach Maloney (and were tremendously grateful for all that he had done for them), but they felt the need to have a fresh perspective.

Because they wanted to finish out their semester at the University of Wisconsin (after all, Paul had said he didn't want to be a lifelong student), Paul and Morgan made arrangements to train with one of the assistant coaches that they had worked with at Swiss Turners, Andrei Kai, at a nearby gym. That way they could complete their schoolwork and then make a move.

The Hamms had been in a lot of gyms

around the country. Through their participation on the national team they knew and had worked out with just about all of the top coaches in the country. They considered their decision about where to go very carefully because, in an Olympic year, they were already taking a risk to make a change like this. They wanted to be sure they made a good choice.

After exploring their options, they decided to move to Columbus to train with Miles Avery, the coach at Ohio State University. The twins considered a number of factors, including the fact that their friend Blaine Wilson was there, along with the talented Raj Bhavsar and Jason Furr, too.

For all of their lives, the Hamms had always been the best gymnasts in the gym. Aside from Coach Maloney, there had only been Paul to push and inspire Morgan and only Morgan to push and inspire Paul. Now they would have a number of top-notch gymnasts to work out with, watch, and get help from. That was something that could only help them reach their peak.

Though working under Coach Avery would be a new experience for the twins, Avery wasn't an unknown. He had been part of the coaching staff at several of the international meets they had been to, and Paul said they liked his style of quietly leading gymnasts where he thought they should be.

Morgan and Paul had worked out with Blaine for years. They had trained together at a number of national and international meets and spent two months together on the T.J. Maxx tour. Paul had tremendous respect for Blaine, and when they had talked to him about moving, he had enthusiastically encouraged them to come and work with him and the others at Ohio State. Not only would the Hamms benefit from being in a gym with other athletes, Blaine knew that having the Hamms in the gym with him would only make him work harder, and he welcomed them.

On top of everything else, the facility at Ohio State, which had just opened in 2002, had been described as the best in the country, complete with a medical staff to help keep the athletes in the best of shape. The Hamms couldn't have looked for anything else in a gym.

It was hard for the twins to move 500 miles away from home; despite all their travel, they had always lived near their parents and enjoyed spending time with them. But when they weighed all the factors, they felt like going to Ohio State was the right decision for them. They moved in January and got right down to work at the gym and enrolled in a light schedule of classes.

Of course a big change like that would take time to adjust to, but the Hamms felt like they fit in well at their new gym. Paul pointed out that the one thing that *hadn't* changed was that he still woke up every morning sore and tired!

Sore or not, the twins were looking forward to going to a few meets with their new coaches. And the 2004 Winter Cup was rolling right up on them in February. They were happy to get back to competition, even though neither twin was going to do all six events.

Paul had bruised his heel in training, so he was going to pass on competing in floor and vault to give his foot time to recover. As always, when he wasn't able to work on specific events, Paul had worked harder on the others, taking the opportunity to really hone his skills. He had worked heavily on rings, in which he still lagged a little behind as a result of the rehab on his shoulder.

Though the twins weren't in contention for the all-around, both Paul and Morgan had a good meet at the Winter

Cup. Paul finished first on pommel horse and third on parallel bars; Morgan came in right behind his brother with a silver on pommel horse. They were happy to see that they didn't seem to have lost much of their edge as a result of the transition from one coach to another.

The twins were both headed to the Visa American Cup at the end of February, along with Blaine and Jason. The meet was at Madison Square Garden in New York City, and the Hamms were looking forward to performing in that historic setting in front of an enthusiastic New York audience.

Everything was as exciting as the twins had expected as the meet began. The fans knew their gymnastics, and the atmosphere was supercharged, as only a Madison Square Garden crowd can get. The men started on pommel horse, usually not a problem for Paul. But unexpectedly, Paul had a fall midway through his routine. He calmly shook it off and kept going, and luckily the rest of the routine was strong enough that the penalty wasn't too bad: he ended up with a decent 9.100. He was happy to see Morgan put in a great routine—at least one of them had a good rotation. In fact, Morgan's pommel horse, something he had worked hard on, was good enough for an individual event win.

Next they moved on to rings. All eyes were on Blaine Wilson as he began a knockout routine. Then suddenly he grimaced and dropped to the mat, holding his arm in agony. Paul and Morgan exchanged shocked and horrified looks. Blaine, who was one of their closest friends, not to mention a key member of what was sure to be an experienced and capable Olympic team, looked like he had a serious injury. This was nothing short of a disaster!

Obviously they had to continue, but Paul's mind kept going back to how Blaine's injuries would impact his career. Blaine was trying to get to his third Olympics, and then he would probably retire. Paul wondered if there was any hope that Blaine could recover in time to go to Athens.

Despite being as worried for Blaine as his brother, Morgan managed to turn in an excellent floor exercise, winning the event with strong tumbling passes and solid landings.

Paul, who was normally relentlessly strong when he was ahead, could have won the meet if he had nailed his high bar routine, but he missed a release on the high bar, which dropped him to third in the all-around.

Morgan tied for second on the high bar, but a fall from the parallel bars left him with the lowest score in that rotation, and the 8.725 held Morgan to fifth at the end of the meet.

Both Paul and Morgan were somewhat disappointed with their results, but their biggest concern was what Blaine's injury could mean for Blaine and Team USA's hopes in Athens.

It turned out that Blaine had torn his bicep muscle and was headed to Alabama for surgery. Paul and Morgan each had plenty of experience by now with rehab. They both knew what it was like to work to get healthy and how important it was to have someone around to help with the motivation. They were glad they'd be at the Ohio State facility when Blaine got home so they could lend him their support.

Meanwhile, the Hamms needed to continue their competition schedule to stay on track for the Olympics. Less than two weeks after the Visa American Cup, Paul headed to Lyons, France, for a World Cup meet. He turned in a solid performance, though he didn't take home any medals.

Morgan, however, walked away with a gold medal on high bar *and* a silver on the floor exercise at the Siegfried Fischer Trophy FIG World Cup in Rio de Janeiro, Brazil.

With these early international competitions under their belts, the twins, along with Jason Gatson and Steve McCain, headed for the Pacific Alliance meet in Honolulu in mid-April, where they would face teams from eight other nations.

The U.S. team looked strong, overcoming an early deficit to beat Japan and China in the team championship. Paul had a very good meet and collected a lot of hardware. In addition to contributing to the team win, he won gold on high bar and vault, silver on floor exercise, and bronze on pommel horse and parallel bars. He was particularly pleased with his high bar routine, which he had continued to refine, making it easier to hit all the skills. Not to be left out, Morgan beat Paul for the gold on floor and tied him for the pommel horse bronze.

Coach Avery was understandably pleased with his newest athletes, declaring himself a happy coach.

Paul and Morgan were equally satisfied with their new situation—they were right where they wanted to be at that point, training with the coach and the gym mates who they believed could help them the most.

Becoming world champion hadn't taken away from Paul's hunger for Olympic success. If anything, he was more focused on winning in Athens than ever. Of course, if Paul and Morgan wanted to be on the Olympic team, they were going to have to earn their places. Looking ahead to the selection trials in June made even Paul a little nervous. He couldn't get over how many fine athletes with international experience were vying for spots on the U.S. Olympic team. Making the team was the first big hurdle, but the tough competition for team berths would ensure that the U.S. delegation was strong enough to win if they stayed healthy and hit their routines.

One thing was for sure—Paul and Morgan were both confident that the team that traveled to Athens would be a very different team than the one that went to Sydney. This time around, the Hamm twins had plenty of international experience and tons of experience competing with their U.S. Senior teammates. All they could do was hope that the end result would be Olympic gold in Athens in 2004!

Hamm Twins Profile

	Morgan Hamm	Paul Hamm
Hometown	Waukesha, Wisconsin	
Current residence	Columbus, Ohio	
Birthday, place	September 24, 1982, Ashland, Wisconsin	
Club	Team Chevron, Ohio State	
Coaches	Miles Avery, Arnold Kvetenadze, Doug Stibel	
Favorite event	All	
Hobbies	Tennis, playing cards	Tennis
Began gymnastics	1989	
Years on Jr. National team	3 (1996–99)	4 (1995–99)
Years on Sr. National team	4 (2000–present)	5 (1999–present)
Family	Parents Sandy and Cecily, sister Betsy	
Height	5'6"	
Weight	143 lbs	137 lbs

Morgan Hamm Career Highlights

2003 World Championships: team silver medal

2003 U.S. Championships: gold medal, floor exercise

2002 U.S. Championships: gold medal, floor exercise

2001 Pontiac American Team Cup: team gold medal

2000 Olympic Games: member, men's team

Paul Hamm Career Highlights

2003 World Championships: individual gold medal, all-around; team silver medal; gold, floor exercise

2003 U.S. Championships: gold medal, all-around; gold medal, pommel horse; gold medal, high bar; silver medal, floor exercise; silver medal, parallel bars

2002 U.S. Championships: gold medal, all-around; gold medal, pommel horse; gold medal, vault; silver medal, floor exercise

2002 Pacific Alliance Championships: gold medal, team; gold medal, individual all-around; gold medal, vault; gold medal (tie), horizontal bar

2001 World Championships: team silver medal

2001 Pontiac American Team Cup: team gold medal

2000 Olympic Games: member, men's team